CW00832331

Recollections Of Mr Manoly Lascaris

Vrasidas Karalis

EasyRead Large

Copyright Page from the Original Book

All rights reserved. This book is copyright. Apart from any fair dealing for the purposes of study, research, criticism, review, or as otherwise permitted under the Copyright Act, no part may be reproduced or transmitted in any form or by any means, electrical or mechanical, including photocopying, recording, or by any information storage or retrieval system, without permission in writing from the publishers.

The moral right of Vrasidas Karalis to be identified as the author of this work is hereby asserted.

Copyright © Vrasidas Karalis, 2008

Front and back cover photograph: Copyright © William Yang
Front cover: Manoly Lascaris, 'Kitchen, Martin Road, 1990'
Back cover: Patrick White and Manoly Lascaris, 'Martin Road, 1985'

First published by Brandl & Schlesinger in 2008
PO Box 127 Blackheath NSW 2785 Australia
www.brandl.com.au

Cover and book design by András Berkes-Brandl

Australia Council
for the Arts

This project has been assisted by the Commonwealth Government through the Australia Council, its arts funding and advisory body.

National Library of Australia
Cataloguing-in-Publication entry:

Author: Karalis, Vrasidas.
Title: Recollections of Mr Manoly Lascaris / Vrasidas Karalis.
Publisher: Blackheath, NSW: Brandl & Schlesinger, 2008.
ISBN: 9781876040956 (pbk)
Subjects: Karalis, Vrasidas.
Lascaris, Manoly, 1912–2003.
White, Patrick, 1912–1990.
Intellectuals – Australia. Authors, Australian – Intellectual life – 20th century.
Dewey Number: 305.552092

Printed by Trojan Press

TABLE OF CONTENTS

Vrasidas Karalis

Recollections of Mr Manoly Lascaris

Vrasidas Karalis is associate professor in Modern Greek Studies at the University of Sydney. He has published extensively in Greek studies, modern philosophy and aesthetics. He is the editor of *Modern Greek Studies* (Australia and New Zealand). His publications include books on Nikos Kazantzakis and Patrick White. He is the co-editor of two collective volumes on Martin Heidegger and Hannah Arendt. He has received awards for his Greek translations of Patrick White.

To Robert Meader,
home

Foreword and Acknowledgements

Remembering

How can you remember all this?

I am asked of my discussions over seven years with Mr Manoly Lascaris.

I couldn't forget anything. On the contrary, I have had to censor my memories the way those who witness grand figures always do, by simplifying, suppressing, deleting.

Yes, I kept notes. Several months into our encounters, sensing how arresting his words were, and how enchanted I was, they became even more detailed. He chastised me for my 'impoliteness', my 'proletarian inability to concentrate'. 'So uncouth!' he protested to God. 'So graceless. Such bad manners!'

I used his Greek words as an excuse. I was a translator, after all, and working on Patrick White's novels. 'I must look for the meaning of this in the dictionary, Mr Lascaris. Don't take it the wrong way–'

'I hope that you are going to make me into a fictional character,' he said.

'You're too real, Mr Lascaris. I cannot sublimate you.'

'In any case, don't mention anything about our "erotics"; we never made a theatre out of our life.'

'No, don't worry. I hate such stories myself.'

'Deep down, there must be traces of intellect in you!'

I sighed with relief.

For years, I forgot my notes. Other events in my life pushed his memory aside. If I thought of him sometimes, it was to feel really angry with myself for having wasted precious time in search of a superior father figure.

Unfortunately, the destination of our journey is our posthumous life. After Mr Lascaris' death, everything fell into place. Then I could start a dialogue with him, uninterrupted, and without being humiliated. I tried to re-construct, re-live, re-enact. There are words and gestures that I have left out. But his presence, with his slow pace, relentless stream of language and graceful movements, constantly guided me back to the situations we experienced together. In the darkest moments of self-delusion I thought that he might have seen me as his last chance to justify his existence to the world. I never really convinced him of my good intentions, and he was absolutely certain that in the end I would do the wrong thing – again.

I'd like to thank Jane Harrison, Cathy Cassis and Tony Stephens for their comments on the first draft of this book; David Brooks for asking me to translate my initial obituary from the original Greek; Diana Giese, my editor, for her inventive and imaginative interventions in the text; and my publishers and friends Veronica Sumegi and András Berkes-Brandl for their warm acceptance of such a paradoxical publication.

Three sections of the book have been published, in different forms. *Of a certain Greek writer* appeared in *Diavazo* in Athens (2003); *Of things past* in the Greek journal *Hodos Panos* (2003); and *A Byzantine aesthete in Australia* in *Southerly* (2007).

Vrasidas Karalis January 2007–March 2008

January 2007–March 2008

Prelude

'It would have been tactless to talk about myself while Patrick's presence was still in this house,' Manoly Lascaris told me when I presumptuously asked. He didn't want to talk about the past; you just had to accept it.

At first sight, Lascaris was of no consequence – just an obstacle on the way to the great man. He had lived for so long in the shadows of White's life that his smiling face exuded an irritating mystery, an indeterminate quality which puzzled and intrigued. Indeed you met him with the expectation – or even the premonition – that there was something beyond his words which would appear in moments of unexpected clarity, at a time when he was ready to offer graceful hospitality, an entrance to his esoteric world.

'People here call me constantly by my first name. I can't tell you how hurt I feel: such disrespect, impertinence!'

'But why don't you say something?' I asked naïvely.

'It's beneath my rank to raise matters of protocol!' he replied, pressing his lips together.

'Living for so long under the wings of a great writer is a bitter privilege,' he continued. 'Sometimes you don't know if you really exist or have a self, or even if you *are* yourself!'

His monotonous voice became fluid, inflected, broken. You could sense the real man trying to reclaim his position in life. Manoly Lascaris had an acute, almost painful understanding of his place in the 'itinerary of things', as he used to say.

'I am nothing,' he told me once; 'I am nobody, immensely insignificant. Who will ever care if I existed?'

I was very young when we first met. I had just arrived in Australia and fallen in love with Sydney. His words gave me an imaginary map covering the immense amplitude of the city. 'Don't go there,' he would command. 'That is not a place for intellectuals! And you pretend to be one!' Or 'Sydney is a pre-Christian city on the way to conversion; you can be Christianised together.'

I was seduced by his arrow-like, unbending statements; they confused me but also made me feel complete. It took me some time to find my way through them; I was surprised, frustrated, enchanted, resentful all at the same time. Through such conflicting feelings, a different perception of Lascaris gradually emerged for me: that of a man with an archaic mentality who could transform his encounters with people into abstract, geometric lines. *Euclid alone has looked on Beauty bare:* Edna St Vincent Millay wrote the line which encapsulates this.

He understood situations and appreciated individuals from the perspective of whether they were just or unjust, and for him that meant balance. Virtues should balance vices: the purpose of living is to work out your identity through exploring each. Their co-existence, in perpetual tension, gives birth to the dimension of the spiritual in every individual.

'Mankind can be perfected only in profanity,' he told me once, and added: 'That's why we must always strive for the opposite. Goodness is what we miss and we dream of, while living in our middle class self-satisfaction.'

In the beginning I befriended Lascaris because of Patrick White. My ambitious project was to translate White's major works, and I wanted to know as much as possible about him, as background. But Lascaris was extremely reserved.

'Most people want to know about our private life,' he told me, the intonation of his voice pointing at me. 'But there is nothing there to discover. We loved each other and we hated each other. The tension kept us together. We were faithful – but that does not mean much any more. We enjoyed each other's silence; isn't that enough? *We* found it enough, and became happy. Being sufficient is a great heresy in these days of greed and insatiability, no?'

Curiosity became genuine interest. Patrick White vanished to the outer horizons of our conversations. On the other hand, I had met Lascaris just after

4

Patrick's death, and despite the occasional tears and his obvious loneliness, there was a distinct feeling of liberation in the house.

Gradually, the shape of a labyrinthine personality emerged. The breath of the vanished king still hung heavily, but Lascaris' own home was expanding. Its corridors and pathways were multiplying; its dead ends were opening out into infinite space. Years later, as I was recollecting our friendship, I understood how slowly and imperceptibly I had sunk into his Minotauric personality.

I was particularly attracted by his feeling for the Greek language. He spoke incessantly in his 'old language', as he called it, with amazing accuracy, succinctness and brevity. My own florid Greek was constantly under siege. He persistently remarked on my 'peculiar syntax', 'convoluted sentences' and 'tautologies', and made other gracefully offensive observations.

Above all I was given the rare opportunity to tease out the differences between our generations. Because my generation never risked anything; we were given everything – even things we never asked for. We had solutions to problems we didn't know existed, and answers to questions we couldn't articulate. Compared with his generation, we had no intensity of feeling, no economy of action, no sense of private space.

They grew up under tension and fear. Beneath war, persecution, escape. What was our fear? Anxiety? Paranoia? Excitement and welcome thrills in lives swamped by affluence and abundance and comfort? We tried to invent problems out of our good luck, while his generation experienced tragedies that we could not even imagine.

'I belong to the cosmopolitan, serene, geometric eighteenth century,' he said once. 'You are after excitement – because life today is so confusing. Think of us: thrown into two wars, living amid centreless hopes. We had to be strong and faithful. Our dilemmas remained hidden within us; we could not talk about them. I was given no other option. Listen, we must find a common language here. Otherwise we will be lost in our egos.'

His morbid taste for making fun of me even when I had said nothing was something that I can never forget.

A Byzantine aesthete in Australia

Since the 60s that house had been a strange symbol: 20 Martin Road, Centennial Park. After my arrival in Australia, curious yet reluctant, I wanted to see with my own eyes the space populated by Patrick White's imagination and haunted by Manoly Lascaris' shadowy presence.

When I was living in Amsterdam, I had read *Flaws in the Glass* and felt a great desire to see Mr Lascaris, if for no other reason than the latent solidarity all migrants feel when they meet each other, realizing that there is no way back home. It was December 1993, three years after Patrick's death, when I rang the bell after several long exploratory calls.

A short man, well aged, opened the door.

'Welcome,' he said. 'This is our home.' He continued with that most Greek of questions: 'Where are you from?'

'From Olympia, in the Peloponnese,' I replied.

'Oh, you are from the old Greece then,' he said, offering me a chair from the 60s. 'We, the Greeks of Asia Minor and Constantinople, have a mentality completely different from yours. We are made of different *étoffe,* as they used to say in Smyrna.'

A vague Oriental Greek accent reverberated in the atmosphere of that serene house, its furniture covered with the dust of absence and the imperceptible movement of memories. A little dog, Milly, ran joyfully up and down, interrupting the hieratic slowness of his movements. The walls were covered with paintings. In a corner there was a candle under an icon of the Transfiguration of Our Lord, painted by a student of the iconographer Kontoglou. A black rosary hung next to it. 'They stole the authentic Kontoglou icon back in 1973,' he said sadly.

And then he started talking to me in Greek, using archaic expressions and puzzling idioms which to my Athenian ear sounded rather amusing, and speaking ever-faster. He spoke without pause, gazing into my eyes to see if I was following him.

'When I came to Australia in 1949, people here didn't know that tomatoes were for salads. They believed that they were – can you believe it? My God, it was horrible, it was so strange – they believed they were some kind of fruit! Like oranges and apples, for example. And what about oil? Yes, my dear sir! What's your name again? I mean your Christian name? Vrasidas? That's quite unusual, you must admit, eeehh? Was there a saint with that name? Well, let me tell you that, yes, I could buy oil–*buuuut* only, I repeat only, at the chemist's! I speak about the olive oil, of course.'

An Alexandrian dialect, as in Cavafy's poetry, was conquering the house. It was persistent, growing in strength and confidence, as if trying to regain lost territory.

'You know, sir,' he continued in the plural, 'I don't usually speak Greek and I think that I should practise my old language so I won't forget it. On the other hand, I am almost eighty-five years old. I am healthy, yet very close to the grave, as Eleftherios Venizelos used to say. Do you know anything about Venizelos? Do they still talk about him in Greece? We were all Venizelists, despite the fact that our class in Athens and Alexandria were all royalists. Even Cavafy himself, he was a royalist – yes, Cavafy, about whom I have to tell you: he never had a shower in his life! I was a clerk in that bank then – I can't remember which bank now – you understand, after the Catastrophe, we had nothing left. I had to work and make a decent living. He had dealings with us. That must have been in 1928 or maybe 1929? Well, he never washed himself and stank from afar, despite some whiff of cheap perfume on his face! Well, this is what happens, as you know, with all bankrupt bourgeois.'

He hadn't forgotten a thing. His whole life, before the fatal meeting in 1943 that had sent him to the other side of the world, was spinning in his mind as his memory danced, intoxicated by the seduction of a paradise lost somewhere in Port Said. That was where he had his first love affair, so he said – or was it in Alexandria? – where he cried when he found his first love having sex with somebody else. Here was a real-life Marcel Proust in front of me, immobilized by the fragrance of tea, the lust for remembering.

'I saw them,' he told me with immense sadness, 'in my own bed. We Greeks are so shallow and untrustworthy! Very few people know how much I have despised "carnalities" ever since. That was something Patrick under stood very well.'

'Would you like some coffee?' he continued. 'Personally, I've always preferred tea. Since the time we lived in Alexandria, my class drank only tea. Coffee was for the lower classes.'

Athens, Piraeus, Smyrna, Alexandria, Jerusalem, Sydney: all had lost their temporal and spatial dimensions for him and were transformed into one great travelogue within the chaos of his sensual wanderings.

'Some days ago, I had a visit, a count from Poland. He talked with such arrogance: "We belong to the landed gentry. Before the War, we had our own county." "I beg your pardon, sir," I replied. "My family produced the emperors of Byzantium! We were the true heirs of the senatorial families of Rome – not barbarian upstarts!" These people must be taught their proper place, especially here in the colonies,' he continued. 'Can anyone compare the Byzan tine aristocracy with a county in pre-war Poland? *Poland,* of all places! No, certainly, not! They can't be compared–*buuuut* we know a lot about such ambitious snobs: they will do anything to convince the world that their families have existed since time immemorial.'

I wanted to ask him about Patrick. I was then trans latiI was then translating *Voss.* What had he been reading at the time? I dared to ask.

'He read a lot, that man. I can't remember. Rich people enjoy such luxury. My sister in Athens – please don't forget to visit her; she lives in Kolonaki – used to say that books were invented so that people won't look into each others' eyes.'

What was he trying to tell me? Was this the desire of an overlooked man to speak about himself? Or maybe he was now celebrating his liberation from the dynastic presence of someone who had oppressed him for so long? Or perhaps it was the freedom that only your first language can offer, the language of your dreams in which sometimes you can hear your own death talking back to you? *Solitude and old age transformed me into a storyteller,* as Aristotle said.

'Did we love each other? After fifty years of an exclusive relationship, *what is this thing called love?* Isn't that a Greek song? I heard it once on the Australian radio in Greek – and started crying! When we lived in the outback, I used to move around the radio dial just in case the airwaves would bring Greek voices to me. And believe it or not, sometimes I could listen in on the high frequencies to the announcements of the Greek Red Cross, to the names of missing people. It was like a religious revelation to me. I still remember the names of those missing Greeks. In the middle of nowhere a name was a complete story, a connection with people and places back in the deep blue of our sea. Because we must remember that we were emperors of Byzantium. But after *our child* was brutally blinded by that ghastly usurper of the throne, Michael Paleologue, it was inevitable that we would lose our capital and our dominions.'

'Sorry, Mr Lascaris – who was your child?'

'You know nothing about history, that's obvious! I am talking about John Doukas Lascaris, the legal heir to the throne of Constantinople, who was blinded by his own Lord Protector when he was only eleven years old. We remember, of course, that back then the abominable Crusaders held our capital captive. In Nicaea my family established a glorious state – and yet that dreadful individual blinded *our child* so that we lost our throne in 1261. *Buuuut* it was only a matter of time before the price was paid for such an atrocity. In 1453 the Empire was conquered by the Ottomans, and vanished. You must surely know that? God imposes his retribution on the evil-doer and his works. So the Christian Empire fell because of that original crime against my family.'

Seven hundred years later *our child* was still alive in that house in Sydney. So were *our throne, our Empire, our family,* as if nothing had happened in between and there was a direct line of communication with the fatal events of the thirteenth century. I was puzzled, amused, somehow inspired to go back and study the period. When I told him so, he replied, with contempt in his voice:

'You didn't know anything about this? What are they teaching you at school nowadays?'

And he forged on: 'I have some kind Greek neighbours. Now that I am left alone, they remember me every Christmas and Easter, and bring me Oriental sweets. The other night as I was taking Milly out for a walk, I fell down on the footpath. I was all covered in blood, unable to get up – until a stranger helped me. One of the minor tragedies of my everyday life: alone at night on the ground, covered in blood. It was a rather pitiful sight. And believe it or not, my dear friend, even in that situation I had a tune running through my mind – yes, strange as it sounds, I was silently singing the national anthem of Greece, something that I have never done before. Quite strange! *Buuuut* it is quite a catchy tune, you must admit!'

I had to go. It was already very late, and quite hot and humid. December 1993. Several days later huge bushfires set ablaze a large area around Sydney.

'You must come back,' he said, with sadness in his voice. 'Feel free to visit me whenever you want. I will tell you some interesting stories about living in the 50s and 60s in this country. Give me your word.'

I visited him many times during the 90s. He told me stories about his life and the lives of others, with sensitivity, discretion and deep respect for their privacy. Occasionally he changed his entire style of talk to make some spectacularly vulgar comment.

'Don't forget that Alexandria and Smyrna were notorious ports,' he told me. 'I learned the argot of sailors and wharfies in my youth. *Buuuut* I have never betrayed my class: our family gave me solid principles which I brought with me to the Antipodes. Please come back soon: what survives is language and Greek words give me strength. It is like going to church! For all of us immigrants, our native language is the only church in which we can venerate the absent deity. Sometimes in my dreams, I see Patrick talking to me in Greek! And he sounds so beautiful. Language and love in the same dream! Why did I have to travel so far away in order to experience such unity? And at such an age? We are so mysterious, we humans! Before we die, we will feel that all these things happened to someone else, and that our real life begins then. But it will be too late. Come and visit me again, as often as you like. But please avoid Oxford Street, one of the temptations of Sydney: very few people realize how easily history can regress to horrible prejudices and persecutions. Stay vigilant and give your heart to anything that will talk back to you in your dreams. This is the only redemption we can hope for.'

He retained the tendency to the didactic until the very end of our friendship.

Of things past

I visited Mr Lascaris almost every month for over seven years. Our meetings were frequent, especially between 1994 and 1997. He read my translation of *Voss,* made some polite approving comments but then told me in passing that my language was 'rather irregular', whereas Patrick's was a model of stylistic perfection.

'This is not what I have read in the reviews of his novels!' I ventured.

He gave me another stoic smile, and started a long diatribe about posthumous fame.

'A writer,' he said, 'must create *sub specie aeternitatis.* If he satisfies the readers of his own age, I am afraid he will be condemned by those of two generations later. Remember Shakespeare! Remember Dante! Alternatively, he will be liked by his contemporaries, but for the wrong reasons. Proust was rejected by Gide – of all people! (What a facile writer – such silly re-inventions of Greek myths.) But look what happens today.'

He took a deep breath.

'Can't you see: Patrick's writing must be rejected by this generation, even by the next one, so that new writers will feel free and liberated from the shadow of heavy paternal authority. They will try to transcend their immediate fathers and search for spiritual links with the past. We must rescue great writers from oblivion when they are not supported by any structure of power or the cultural system. In one hundred years, a sensitive mind will be able to revisit Patrick's work and relive its intensity. People today read through the summary reviews in the newspapers – but how can you give a synopsis of his novels? How can you translate his sentences into familiar ghosts and domesticated demons? You can't do that without losing the main thrust of his *mythos.* It has one sole purpose: to upset, disturb and alienate. Of course he had money and didn't care for popularity. But his heart was in the right place: he was prepared to be forgotten.'

'You are speaking like an oracle, Mr Lascaris,' I said.

'Well,' he replied, 'I was always tempted by loneliness towards megalomania! On the other hand I must never forget my classical education and the need to see life through fragile eyes. If St Paul said anything good, it was that *power becomes perfect in weakness.* That's what I feel like myself: weak, fragile, vulnerable. My creature-hood overpowers my mind and self-confidence. It is through this that I can read Patrick's novels, searching for a brief glimpse of kindness, as he himself would have said. In the most miserable moments of my life I used to close my eyes and remember the Mediterranean blue which nurtured my senses back then. I can still hear the endless murmuring of the waves along the shores of Egypt where I first felt my body and my conscience in action.'

'What are your recollections from that period?' I asked in the most clinical way.

'There was that beautiful German officer in Port Said: tall, slender, with dreamy eyes, naked against the setting sun. I was crushed by the density of his body; I felt small and insignificant before such cruel beauty, so tangible, so overpowering. I felt like an intruder into existence after I touched his porcelain skin which reflected the sun like a living statue. Years later, in 1936 or 1937, after Hitler took over, he sent me a desperate letter from Germany. I kept it with me for years; I even brought it to Australia where I lost it somehow, at Castle Hill. In it he asked me to send him an invitation to Egypt; otherwise, he would be arrested, he wrote. I was young and thought that he exaggerated. I never heard from him again. Who knows what happened to those beautiful lips, that magnificent luminous skin? I think that this is a poem by Cavafy, isn't it?'

'That's a very tragic story,' I said. 'By then Hitler had made very clear what he was going to do.'

'I know,' he said melancholically. 'We never forget the guilt that places us in history, no? When we realize our historical moment, guilt emerges in us. Things we didn't do; words we never spoke; invitations we never made. Guilt makes us live in history. Even you, young man, full of the arrogance of your relativism and the indifference of your self-sufficiency: you must discover your own guilt. Old age shows you nothing else but how to smile at yourself. One day the waves of history bring you ashore on distant land where no memories can be rekindled, and you have to populate the place with forms, shadows and myths that will tame their strangeness and transform their immensity.'

Had I said anything?

Another deep breath.

'Patrick's novels did exactly that: they projected on to the immense depths of this land the myths of human adventures and human failures. They humanized space; emptiness became meaningful; the distant lost its sharpness; the invisible became the dance of fearsome colours. I was there, my young friend, and I heard Patrick moan over his discoveries and cry for the incompleteness of his vision.'

'Mr Lascaris,' I whispered, 'you present Patrick as some kind of prophet.'

'People think of prophets and mystics as otherworldly creatures,' he continued vehemently, 'as in popular movies or the grandly boring novels of Dostoevsky. Patrick was the prophet of the mundane, the ordinary, the trivial, which had to be announced in order to be seen. His works annunciate things with their mission, as in the Gospel story of Mary. Why are we so prone to leaving the things we desire the most undone? Just sketches, some hints, some notes, fragments of a map destroyed by our curiosity and inventiveness.'

Again a deep breath.

'If I like something in Patrick's novels, it is their unmediated perception of the real. Yet he never became vulgar or petty or base, even though the real is all of the above, plus the conscience that perceives it. And we can't cope effectively with the contents of our conscience, so we turn to the novels of today in order to feel good – even if they describe or profess to describe something bad.'

'This is an over-simplification, Mr Lascaris,' I dared to interrupt.

He raised his hand in a commanding way and kept talking:

'Patrick's novels belong to the classical tradition of forms finding their origin, as in *The Iliad:* the inanimate world is objectively active in them. Modern novels falsify reality because they bring the writer to the fore as someone who has decided never to grow up. He interposes himself between us and the world he describes, like a child gesticulating and shouting to be noticed. So they portray a universe in constant conflict with itself; they show no gratitude and wonderment for the great luck of being here and seeing the radiance of things: the stars, the trees, the sea and the humans. Patrick thought that our weakness, our vile character, our misery may lead to what creates goodness in life. This is a morality which cannot be digested by the middle class, the professional religious people and the philosophers of naïve meliorism. As a matter of fact he himself couldn't accept his own discovery, and that made his mind so interesting, so unpredictable and so lonely. Do we ever accept our greatest truths? No, definitely not! Because we cannot see beyond our contradictions. Somebody else makes our truths active reality.'

All these words were said in Greek; and that word *meliorism,* which I had never heard before! It was really astonishing how deep and active his bond was with his 'old' language. I was never able to see if he was the same with other people, especially in English. He avoided bringing his friends together or meeting them at the same time. I never understood why.

'That was so amazing, Mr Lascaris,' I said. 'I wish I could write as you speak.'

'It is because you want to write as you speak that you are unable to write at all!' he replied.

'Please, as the Gospel says, help me in my unfaithfulness!'

'Such a good thing to be unfaithful!' he sighed, clasping his hands. 'It helps sort out your mind against the background of confusing multiplicity. Yet, I must remind you of an old truth: we are motivated by desire and end up living our desire in terror. Ultimately, what we achieve becomes our punishment.'

He hesitated. Then:

'Small stories give great promises: two people talking about something beyond themselves. That's a promise. Let's meet often.'

'Mr Lascaris,' I said, my voice quavering. 'Promises begin at home – although where is home for a nomad like me? I really don't know–'

'My friend,' he said, 'you are so lucky not to have been touched by my sense of irony. And I am very lucky to experience through you my second childhood, before dying.'

I didn't understand what he meant. But I was learning so many threatening Greek words from him.

It was as if he never lost his way, never faltered, never went against his better nature. His hands moving up and down, writing admonitions on invisible parchment.

Oh, his polysyllabic Greek words! Swords of revenge against my reality.

Lost objects

It was raining in Sydney. Then there was scorching sun. After a while, for several hours, fog covered the city. The skyline disappeared. People were like wet plastic animals moving aimlessly. The sun came out again. I closed my eyes and remembered the snowy redemptive monotony of Russia, Finland, Holland.

I was translating *A Cheery Soul.* Translator's dilemma: how do we render into Greek *'dog is "God" turned around'* – and the rest? How do we turn into another language Australian colloquialisms? Thankless, time consuming, mind-devouring task: pizza, cholesterol, self-hypnosis were the only ways out. The phone rang.

His voice:

'You have disappeared, Mr Vrasidas.'

'I'm sorry,' I replied, somehow embarrassed, 'but I have so much to do. Plus some family problems back there. And last but not least that play by Patrick. Why did he write plays? There is no tragic sentiment today. Language cannot give birth to confrontation with our destiny. Why did he write plays?'

Long silence. Was he bored by this and similar questions? Or maybe he was trying to find the right answer? Then as usual he started talking about something completely different.

'You know,' he said rolling the Greek word *xerrrreteeee* on his lips, 'you know, prose is always sad and sober, whereas poetry implies an element of jocularity. Prose always poses problems of style, of rhythm, of punctuation. Poetry is like the accordion: you can suspend it and close it as many times as you like, especially today. For Patrick, theatre was a hybrid state between soberness and frivolity. I thought that sometimes he overdid it. But where he is successful, you must admit that his words breathe like tangible beings. You know, deep down Patrick was a religious personality, so he was prone to turning romantic, especially when he was pretending to hate romanticism. But he always started with complexities and ended with terrifying simple truths. Theatre gave him the faces of actors so that everything would seem normal – even when the normal was an awesome threat.'

'I can't follow you,' said. 'You are so elliptical today, so fragmented. Is everything fine?'

'Perceptive – that's really unusual for a Greek! I am not a critic, as you know, *buuuut–*' he laughed ironically, 'I remembered today when I last saw my mother as a child. The weather brought back that hazy feeling of old fragrances, clothes, rooms, shoes. You understand: the colour and the texture of lost objects. I suppose that in some instances we must ask ourselves the crucially stupid question *Where am I?*– and when you ask something like that, you must be in a state of confusion.'

He took a deep breath. He was encouraging himself.

'It has nothing to do with memories, or nostalgia. It simply means *How did I get here?* Sydney is the metropolis of solitude. In Alexandria you didn't have the time to feel alone; you *couldn't* be alone; you were swimming in an endless sea of encounters. But Sydney is different. I've lived here for most of my life now and I think that I know the truth. It's the city of loners – strictly speaking, of orphans. It is a city inhabited by children, innocent, un suspicious, sinless, living in utter solitude. Can I tell you something? Well, these children commit sins because they want to cease being alone; they want to be noticed, recognized, seen! And the worst of all is that they cannot say the simple sentence: "Look at me, I exist!" And I will tell you something more, because you have to grow up at a certain point in your life–'

Did I open my mouth?

'Only when we commit sins, we are seen by God, or his messengers. Because our sins are what really belong to us and express our humanity. Good things come from above: this is from a chant in our Church.'

I remained nailed and frozen.

He went on.

'But in order to be seen by God, you have to be overlooked by people. Yet few people understand this since we don't have a proper vocabulary for loneliness in English, and even I myself don't know that vocabulary in Greek. Struggling to speak about a situation for which we don't possess the vocabulary: it is really indicative of our relationship with God, no?'

Annoying winds were hissing outside like snakes in a garden.

'I will never finish that translation,' I said to myself, 'and what is all this Godtalk?'

And then, as if his voice was going back to correct an error, he called out, exasperated: '*Buuuut* then what is sin? I don't like such Russian "accursed questions". Can a child commit sinful acts? Morality means the right moment to do something – even something which is not good. Anything we do which is not complete is sinful. *Ripeness is all,* as the poet said. These lonely children of Sydney wait for the price of the atonement they have to make. They don't know that it comes for free, in a moment of recognition of what or who stands in front of you. Patrick's novels show exactly that: although you look for redemption in excess or self-punishment, it is given to us in moments of unforseen lucidity. When a stone retains it stone-ness after it has hit you on the head! We all know it can never change – only after we have been hit!'

He took another deep breath; he was calming down, I thought.

He continued relentlessly: 'Last night I dreamed that I was standing in the middle of the Egyptian desert.

In front of me were some soldiers being punished for some strange crime they had committed. "What did they do?" I asked. "It's top secret!" an officer shouted at me. Two of them were lying on the sand and crying with shame. One turned to me and, with tears all over his face, whispered: "Take this picture with you wherever you go." His mouth was full of sand. The other soldiers starting spitting on the two, shouting abuse and calling them vile names. I stepped back. I couldn't do anything. I was afraid; I wanted to run away. The sun was burning my face. But I turned back and said to that man: "I won't forget. I will take your picture with me wherever I go." Then I started running away as fast as I could. I stumbled on a stone, fell to the ground. Soon I felt the aggressive alcoholic breath of the other soldiers, all over me. "Why did you run away?" they were shouting. "Why didn't you spit on them too?" I couldn't say a word; I felt that I would be next. Then I looked around and suddenly they were all gone. In the middle of the desert even the presence of such vile men was a blessing. But now I was alone with only sand in my mouth. I woke up. Milly was licking my hand.'

'Very symbolic dream,' I said.

'Thank God,' he sighed, 'that I can say all these things in Greek – because I feel that whatever I say in English hides half my face.'

We were on the phone for over an hour.

'Modern epics should be called telephoniads,' I said. 'They preserve an ancient oral tradition, you know.'

'Telephoniad?' he exclaimed. 'What a silly neologism! Is this the way they use Greek these days? You must start reading the classics again! In the *o-ri-gi-nal.* This will be the only way to be cured of your horrible pleonasms!'

It was a very common word for students of my generation. Come on!

'When did you finish school in Greece?' he continued. 'Did you really finish studying at the University? Well, I must tell you, you sound very – very – how should I say it? Yes, yes – primitive. You must do something about this.'

I felt he had killed me. Trying to be funny, I said: 'Mr Lascaris, thank God you are not my father.'

To which he replied: 'No, my dear boy, I have to thank God for that.'

It took me several weeks to call him back.

The translation

The Prime Minister was Paul Keating. Several weeks earlier he had declared that the Greeks 'gave Australia her soul': a seductive statement, so woefully untrue! Mr Lascaris said:

'Have you seen Jim Sharman's movie *The Night, the Prowler?* It is an unrecognized masterpiece! Patrick wrote the script and placed three Greeks in Centennial Park singing about planting stones where a woman's heart should be. Well, that's what we did! You know my friend, people fall victim to their own virtues. Our vices give perspective and life-long commitment. You must see that movie.'

'Mr Lascaris,' I replied, 'I have already seen it on Greek television, back in the early 80s. I was deeply impressed – especially by its profane secularity. Her face at the end of the movie, like Garbo's in *Queen Christina*– as Patrick wrote, in a 'state of illumination'. Despite its shortcomings, a wonderful movie.'

'Well, perfection is not a very pleasant experience – you must know that by now. You're almost forty. What makes us complete is our sense of responsibility to others. At a certain stage you feel that your body is betraying you and only then do you realize that all our lives we worship frail transitory gods – and that's happiness. Now if the Greeks gave Australia her soul, this cannot be good in any way. I can't think of any

Greek virtue that could be infused into the body of this country – and as you know, I detest screaming metaphors. Those who feel left out are resentful of the successes of others. I think we must feel happy that other people succeed where we fail and, most importantly, feel grateful.'

'This is so true, Mr Lascaris,' I said. 'I have experienced that realization recently and felt really bad. We Greeks simply have doleful voices which make us look deep and somehow spiritual. It's really sad.'

'It's not only that,' he said. 'We can never repent. I don't think that any human has ever repented, with the exception of St Paul – and we must admit that the fruits of his repentance were not always good, no? But we Greeks lack an internal life, the soul stuff, the stuff of personal history. You know that although I have tried many times, I've never found any autobiographies in Greek? This is really sad: no interiority, no internal conflicts, no sense of the dichotomy within us.'

He stopped and cleared his nose with his archaic handkerchief, after a long search in his fathomless pockets.

'That's what I liked in Patrick and indeed what I like in the Anglo-Saxon character,' he continued. 'That frightening interiority, full of moral dilemmas and guilty secrets. We Mediterraneans have been devastated by the blue serenity of our childhoods. Even if we went through disasters and catastrophes we have remained untouched by history, by the results of our own works. Hence we can never repent. The same applies to the Italians, and even the Arabs. We are all similarly shallow.'

'You're so right,' I whispered. 'That's what I liked in Patrick's autobiography: the inner conflicts leaping out of pages full of complex consequences, of sudden and painful realizations of the qualities of his self. Even his irony is an act of penitence.'

'Identity means visibility, my shallow fellow Greek. Your identity is what can be seen of you. The hidden part of yourself will be revealed when you won't be around to upset it. That's what Patrick did in that book – which very few understood – and that was what he wanted. He didn't want to justify or explain or elucidate our life. He gave a story of his body's movements in time. Our body is existence: such awareness throws most people into panic. But he had the courage to look in the mirror knowing that he was something beyond the total sum of his works and deeds, that he was something more to me and to other people he loved or who loved him. Let's say he never suffered the paralyzing anxiety for recognition. Isn't this enough?'

'Well for us Greeks it isn't!'

'We deserved what we got in the twentieth century. I'm telling you, we are so a-historical, so pre-historic. Australians in their innocence are not as pre-political as we are. They tamed a land, they committed the crimes, as your Keating said, they separated the families from the land. They have every right to create now, because they are motivated by the need to be forgiven for their own actions. This is great, my shallow friend, this is really sublime! I envy them. I stayed in Australia because Patrick brought me to a land whose sun was full of secrets and fears. The Australian sun does not reveal anything; it exposes human conscience to danger. Read *Voss.*'

'Translating that book is a painful experience,' I dared to say.

'Because you are shallow and cannot think! Forget the characters in the book. Pay attention to how Patrick depicts the sun in that saga of exploration. Then you will feel sorry for the Graham Greenes, Lawrence Durrells, Herman Hesses, Thomas Manns or Pasternaks of this world. Not to mention our very own Nikos Kazantzakis, whose Zorba will be the eternal disgrace of the Hellenic language!'

'You are very harsh, Mr Lascaris,' I said, feeling his agitation. I had already published a long book on Kazantzakis.

I diverted him. 'Graham Greene is a very interesting writer, don't you think?'

'I never read his work, although I think I skipped through that cute story about the miracle and the birthmark.'

'Mr Lascaris,' I exclaimed, 'you are unfair, I think.'

'Only truthful,' he said abruptly. 'Now I must go and do some housework. The worst thing for your sanity and commonsense is to believe what Keating said. In order to give soul, you must have soul; and we know that this is not the case with us. We invented tragedy but we constantly play operetta. I suppose this can be called our tragedy!'

I was still young and under the influence of my mother. I was deeply annoyed. I avoided him for weeks. Meanwhile I finished my translation of *Voss*. My publisher in Athens was not impressed. He asked if I had forgotten my Greek.

When some five months later I had the finished translation, I visited Mr Lascaris.

He took it in his hands and noticed that I had written an introduction about their life.

'I hope you don't mention anything explicit about our *erotics*,' he said. 'You know I still have family in Greece and I don't want to embarrass them.'

I drank the instant coffee he offered me, in silence. He started talking about his surviving family and the prospects of the Lascaris as an imperial dynasty.

'We are one of the very few surviving imperial families, you know. There are certain things that we can never lose.'

'But there are no empires today, Mr Lascaris!' I said in exasperation.

'Don't you believe in historical cycles? Things come and go. We will be back to reclaim our position.'

That day he was wearing a pair of prehistoric trousers, a shirt from the Bronze Age, a cardigan from classical times and slippers from the late Middle Ages or Pakistan. I wanted to laugh. It was as if I had met Don Quixote. And then:

'Deep down we are only after an echo. By searching for that echo we can resurrect ourselves in the eternity of symbols. Oh, yes, yes – we grow old and tend to forget that only the echo of an old message can give perspective to our existence. But an echo also means distance and nostalgia: only through them can the injustices of history be appeased.'

His face was immensely sad, like Christ's in Rubliev's icon. He took off his glasses, thick, heavy, ancient.

'But maybe all these are fantasies and delusions and I really have nothing to do with that family and that past. I must tell you that sometimes this secret thought keeps me awake at night. But there is a certain nobility and magnanimity in the belief itself that even proletarians can feel! We want the things we already have, isn't that so? Magnanimity, what a beautiful word in our language! You know, young man, that if you change two letters it means something extremely vulgar – in ancient Greek certainly...'

He pronounced the word in ancient Greek. I didn't know it. Then he translated it into the most obscene word I had ever heard. It was so unexpected that it somehow detached me from the tense atmosphere.

The book, a thick volume of seven hundred pages, was lying on the table between us. It both united and separated us.

'What sort of paper do they use in Greece?' he complained, feeling it. 'Their books are like bricks!' Silence.

'And don't think that I've forgotten what you said about Graham Greene. When you grow up, you must explain it to me.'

When I grow up? He wants me to remain an infant for all time. Plus: I have never finished any book by Greene. Great script-writer for movies, but as a novelist rather lame.

The dream

Several days after I gave him the copy of *Voss,* after the usual niceties, he told me about a dream of his.

'In the dream, I saw myself in this house. The doorbell rang; I opened it and saw a tall, bulky, man who looked like Gough Whitlam on the doorstep. He had no face. He made his way in. Patrick started shouting that faceless people are demons. "We are descending into hell!" he kept screaming. The man who looked like Whitlam stretched out his hand and with his finger pointed to the icons hanging on the walls. I felt that my heart was burning. A solemn tune sounding like Mahler's Fifth Symphony began. "We must finish what we started," Whitlam said. Then his face came into focus. "We must finish what we started," he repeated. Then the whole room evaporated; Patrick and I were hovering in empty space. Whitlam then appeared in royal regalia and kept talking about Classical Athens. "I will be back one day," he proclaimed. Then space started crumbling into little pebbles. My father's face appeared: dark, smiling, cannibalistic. He started wrestling with Patrick as in the ancient games; their bodies were naked and oily. They gasped and hissed. I started crying. "Stop it," I shouted. "Stop it." Then I fainted without seeing what happened.'

A long pause. Diffuse the tension!

'Lots of mystical undertones, Mr Lascaris,' I said.

'We have our moments too,' he replied, shrugging his shoulders.

'How do you explain the wrestling between your father and Patrick?'

'Your questions are a waste of precious symbols!' he exclaimed, and laughed loudly. 'Please do not psychoanalyze me! I've never been able to find the inner self within me, not in my whole life. And you know why? Because I was always at peace with myself! You have to conquer the space of your soul, you know. It is not something given. On the other hand, trying to define yourself is a very funny enterprise, you must agree. Fortunately, we are all so wrong about ourselves! And are so unhappy when we *are* ourselves! When you are yourself, you become an idol to your own mind, in the religious sense of the word. And by becoming an idol, you immediately lose contact with your soul. Only love can bridge the gap: we find ourselves through somebody else. *Buuuut–* you must remember that love is never the answer; love only poses questions. You remain suspended in time and space waiting for the moment of meeting with somebody who will show you the problem.' He paused. 'Is this too abstract for you?'

'No, no,' I said, 'but you must admit you are a bit heavy-duty, as Australians say.'

'That's a low-class expression which you must never use when you are with me!'

'I'm sorry, Mr Lascaris,' I whispered. 'I thought that by now we were beyond such barriers of self-consciousness.'

He softened his face.

'Let's move on,' he breathed heavily. He had made up his mind: I was beyond repair.

'Dreams exhaust my consciousness, you know. I feel that I have lost something valuable when I talk about my dreams. It is that burden of language which makes life a constant conflict with our senses. We lose so much when we talk. We lose our self every time we try to bring it out through language.'

He was sweating. His hands were wet. His forehead was shining with countless drops of sweat. After an eternity of searching, he took out of his depthless pocket a white handkerchief and wiped his brow. He went on:

'Deep down, I don't really like talking. My silence always expressed the best part of my thoughts. Patrick knew that, and treated my silence as a statement of ideas. Love makes silence meaningful. On the other hand, it was immoral to live amidst so much intellect. To be happy and know it is probably to most horrible manifestation of hubris.'

This was a good moment for a question that had lurked in my mind for a long time.

'Mr Lascaris, I am really curious to know – I mean in a good way curious – why you've never written anything yourself–'

Tense and pregnant silence. He replied without even looking at me.

'Writing is a great trap. We must find a reason to write. I was never a romantic. I viscerally detested the seduction of self-pity and the narcissism of victimhood. I didn't want to write anything about myself, you know. Nothing at all. Everything I lived belonged to me and the moment in time I embodied. Something or someone enters your history at a certain stage and redeems your expectations. It happened. I've been happy to remain silent ever since.'

His eyes became moist; there was a catch in his voice.

'I would have liked to have written down my dreams,' he added in a low voice. 'They are the only symptoms of my mental life that can reveal something about me.'

He stopped then, and added violently, hands up and down:

'But who cares? Who would ever care for a life of sheltered insignificance? Who would be interested in the life of a poor and fallen aristocrat? Only romantics

– and I hate them. I am condemned to becoming the ultimate sacrifice of my anti-romanticism, destined to be rescued from oblivion by the romantic cult of the wasted genius. It is Gothic. It is macabre. My personal tragedy.'

He turned, looked sternly at me, and said:

'I hate your superlatives. You talk as if there is no regular size in life. Don't you understand that you underestimate the specificity of things and humans when you project them to such magnitude?'

Where did that come from? Too much mental alternation in one day.

'Mr Lascaris, I have to go. But can I call you back later tonight?'

'No, no,' he replied. 'Come and see me tomorrow. I have so much to tell you about silence.' Then burst into demonic laughter.

For a Greek, he was so untheatrical. And I was definitely beyond repair.

Designed by Chekhov

It was a glorious Sunday, March 1995. The sun was bright, palpable, promising. I made the mistake of taking a silly friend with me.

Lascaris was amused. He was moving slowly. 'Arthritis,' he said. 'Nature punishes my intellect.'

The intruder had come along for gossip – which I should have suspected. After several hours, having heard nothing, he yawned and yawned and felt unwanted. Lascaris remained aloof, almost compassionate. After this person decided to go, he said:

'Yesterday we were talking about writers.'

'That was some months ago, Mr Lascaris,' I said, 'and I know that you don't like talking about such things.'

'Well, I must tell you that I never liked the writers Patrick preferred – for example, Dostoevsky or Tolstoy, despite the fact that the first had written *Crime and Punishment,* a very Christian, therefore contradictory book, and the other *Anna Karenina*– which I never managed to finish, although to this day I live with the inner urge to read it from cover to cover. *Buuuut*– my kindred spirit was always Anton Chekhov. He is modest, refined and balanced. He never overstated anything. He knew when to put a full stop to end his sentences. He knew that literature is a matter of punctuation, and as such it creates its characters through what it conceals, circumvents and omits. He can be found in the punctuation of his writings. I like that kind of elliptical writing, because it is like my own self.'

His was wagging his finger in front of my eyes in a didactic manner.

'You must admit,' I said, 'that sometimes you are very hard to follow, as if you yourself are searching for your identity. Isn't this what Chekhov's characters are doing? You appear secretive and remote, but I know that only people with extreme self-confidence can look for their own selves without being terrorized by the prospect of thinking and feeling for themselves.'

'Muddled thinking, young man,' he sighed. 'You are perceptive, but you see only half-truths. To each of us our own character is our deepest fear. Or should I call it enigma? Socrates said that we have to know ourselves – but I seriously doubt we want to. I think that we have to force our real self to come out into the light of our conscience, by getting rid of habits, customs and routines. Whatever we think of as really ours is in fact our greatest deceiver. When we stand alone at the centre of life's complexity, without our cultural reinforcements, then we can say "I exist".'

'Did you ever succeed in this?'

'I can't really tell. As I've said, our character is our darkest secret. Our main anxiety is that it may be revealed one day. And who wants to feel afraid of his own self? Anyhow, I must have given you an ambiguous impression. I always give that.'

'This is interesting,' I thought. 'Self-criticism.'

'Be honest,' he went on. 'You can't really tell if I am clever or stupid, or whether I lived with Patrick out of a deep sense of inferiority or from fear of coping with my life back home. You can't really tell if my arrival in Australia was a personal mistake, and whether Patrick pitied me, keeping me here because of his philanthropic Protestant sense of responsibility.'

'That's true,' I replied. 'You can't.'

The moment was dense and electrifying. His eyes blinked; my shoulders sagged. Our body language was heavier than our words. Milly danced between us in a barking frenzy. She wanted to play, and we could only talk about human intentions. He put her on his lap and started patting her back; he was elegant, sorrowful, breathing heavily. She calmed down. He said:

'Well, I never found the time to know myself. Patrick talked somewhere about my "immense moral strength". I must tell you that I was always weak and irresolute. In Greek the word *adynamia* describes my existence better than anything else. Because I lived through my powerlessness (such an unmusical word!), and in there I could be safe. It's paradoxical isn't it? My *adynamia* was always my only refuge; I was defenceless, vulnerable, if you like, *because* I felt powerless. I never tried to dominate anything or anyone. Yet this translated our life into an internal journey of exploration among ordinary objects. Some people would say that this was self-exploration and therefore subjectivism and the like. But I feel that in my life, for what it's worth, I was exploring both Patrick and Australia, and there were some interesting people, some curious episodes, some paradoxes, let's say, along the way. Through my *adynamia* I could see the others clearly without projections. They never felt threatened by me. I gave them space to talk and made small gestures of goodwill and offered unnoticed acts of consideration. So I remained hidden – and this is not always bad.'

'But didn't you sometimes feel disregarded or overlooked? How could you face the idea that people thought that you were Patrick's "housekeeper", for example?'

'I didn't really mind. It was, I might say, an amusing misperception. Some newspapers wrote bad things about us, especially after the Prize, and about me, after he died. How can I forget that arrogant painter and his cartoon? But I didn't really care. I knew I was part of something important. It was not about literature or some other cultural invention. I don't think that Patrick wrote real novels. Patrick saved words from oblivion. If I may say so, he saved idioms from falling into non-existence. And this is unforgivable

– for people who don't know the importance of transgression, that is.'

'This is really cool,' I said in English.

'No,' he replied, 'it is really hot today. Humid. Would you like something refreshing?'

Talking about idioms, I said to myself, irritated. 'No, no thank you,' I mumbled. 'Let's return to Chekhov.'

'Oh yes,' he remembered. 'He died young, of tuberculosis, as you may know. Living with illness makes you more perceptive and open to human frailty. Remember Proust and to a certain degree Lawrence or Stevenson. At least we were given the time to redeem ourselves. They were deprived of the simple luxury of being at home in the world. You ask me about leaving Greek seas and arriving in the Antipodean ocean? Who cares? I definitely didn't.'

He stopped, and closed his eyes.

'In my youth, I experienced no youth,' he said, opening his eyes wide behind his terrifying glasses. 'My only conclusion from life concerns the unpredictability of things – which is banal and trite but bitterly true. On the other hand, being an immigrant yourself, you must know that only outsiders have answers to the inside questions of any society or class. And our position as outsiders is to remain where we are, with occasional incursions to the other side of things. Deep down there is nothing exceptional to reveal, since our inevitable destiny happens by chance – as it happens with all people. By chance we fall into the most necessary traps of our life: love for example, friendship or futile passions.'

'Mr Lascaris, I only asked you about Chekhov,' I protested. 'Please don't frighten me with such horrible moral truths!'

'I told you that I liked his short stories and you keep going on as if you didn't believe me. Be more courteous!'

This is what is generally called *catastrophe* in Greek drama. I was irritated by my inability to break through his fortifications. Milly jumped to the floor and went away to explore an intrusive smell.

'So what about Chekhov?' I said, a bit louder.

'This alone will suffice: his style never made the Universe unfeeling and paralytic. All his works resonate with the many warm, shrill and helpless voices of the situations they describe. In my understanding, this is greatness!'

He paused for breath and added:

'Australia is a country designed by Chekhov; it is sensitivity at its subtlest. Manning Clark thought of Australian history as a cosmic drama of Dostoevskian magnitude but, as in anything he did, he misunderstood his own country. He was too much involved in the business of being Australian. Australians care more for a wounded person than a dead one. They care for the "littleness" of insignificant incidents, rather than for conflicts with destiny on a grand scale. They understand suffering, and engage in small acts of consideration that redeem and liberate in order to alleviate pain and make happiness possible. That's Chekhov – from his very best pages, I must stress.'

He stopped for few seconds, and took a deep breath.

'Is he asthmatic?' I wondered. No, surely not. Arthritis I suspected made his walking heavy and his body struggle. He got up and approached the kitchen door to the pergola at the back.

'Somebody is having a barbecue,' he said, and his voice was full of complaint. 'Can you cook?'

'Oh no,' I replied in embarrassment. 'Whenever I try, something evil comes out, leading to intense suffering in my stomach.'

He said: 'I read somewhere that literature in the new world moves through three unfolding stages: colonial, provincial and metropolitan. I still think that most Australian writers are to this day either in the first or the second stages. They try to re-affirm their identity, which proves that they are still dependent on their origins. Or they maintain a restricted vision of the world by looking through the rear window. The only writer who belongs to the metropolitan stage is Patrick.'

'That's a big statement. You usually avoid such super-assessments.'

'I know: my moderation has been a legend to my own conscience. But let me continue. A metropolitan writer meddles with myths, re-interprets them, re-formulates their message. That's what Patrick did – and he has been punished.'

Then he thought again and summed up:

'Well, I think that Patrick went even further, to the self-reflective stage of unfolding by meditating on the act of writing, as if it were a biological fact which could be analyzed and quantified. At the end of his life he became a Pythagorean! He rejected the Orphic enchantment with surfaces and colours which had earlier fascinated him, and took on the whirlwind of abstract geometries. Writing privileges euphoric frivolity. It was very unfortunate that he went so deep.'

When he uttered such demoralising truths, I knew that I had overstayed. Milly came in again, and he spent most of his time talking to her. I didn't know what to do with my hands: awkwardness.

'Good dog,' he said. 'She knows all too well the importance of human touch.'

Which meant: 'Just get out!'

'You make me so cheerful,' he told me at the door. 'I feel so buoyed up by your questions that I can play with Milly for hours.'

His hands again: up, down, sideways, opening the invisible scrolls of the foundational metropolitan text.

Love

Mr Lascaris said: 'Love never changes anything; it only makes things milder.'

'But you were so faithful to your love!'

'So naïve, young man, so naïve!' he exclaimed. 'I continue: love which is not indulgence – that is, greed or cannibalism – is so rare.'

I insisted: 'How, then, can you remain faithful to something so fluid and so impossible?'

'Poor thing,' he said with immense sadness. 'You are still so in need of your mother. You're still looking for the elusive stability she gave you when you lived among the myths of childhood.'

He laughed. I laughed too.

'Every life shared is a sacrament,' he said, with sudden terrifying seriousness. 'I was struggling to escape from my own family tradition, and love made the pain of separation lighter. Together we explored the goodness of our mortality. Should I say the *transfigurable* elements in us? Because there are things that never change. But even if someone changes, he searches for what he has lost. We lose what we wanted to be lost. And the gap in us makes everything bearable afterwards.'

'Since you were both intellectuals, you could make such a choice.'

'Well, today social classes differ only in the degree of their mental disorder. Their conflicts are merely about the type of treatment they prefer. We belonged to ourselves, young man. We never wanted to condemn ourselves to respectability. Our death will give voice to the silences of our life. Patrick prayed but, as you may know by now, prayer means listening carefully to somebody else's words, sighs and whispers. His prayers were about what I had asked for him, not about his individual wishes.'

'But what made your love last?'

'Men can love one another because they don't know the truth. Let's say that we wanted to test our endurance.'

He used the heart-breaking monastic word *karteria.* His eyes suddenly filled with tears. This threw me. I didn't know what to do with my body, whether or not to look away. After a few minutes, he regained his composure.

'Patrick talks about this in his autobiography: how a relationship outlasts the people who made it real. That's what we did. Because – honestly – in life we simply have to deal with inconsistencies; they give purpose to our self-awareness. And that's what Patrick's novels are about: inconsistencies, and sometimes about coincidences. If I could reduce his work into the geometrical lines that define his characters, I would argue that inconsistency and coincidence give Patrick's work its unity.'

'That's a sweeping generalization, Mr Lascaris. There are so many other things in his works. So much existence, mysticism, poetry–'

'I know that, young man. *Buuuut* you must remember: Patrick was never converted to anything except to organic forms. He enjoyed the skin of things: he described their texture, their density, their colour. Organic forms never fail you. He was religious, yes, a neo-Platonist probably, although that sounds as if it contradicts what I said earlier – but yes. You know, all writers are neo-Platonists. They succumb to the pleasures of seeing, since no appropriate story can be found about the spirit. But Patrick also had plenty of commonsense. That gave him a deeply moral vision of humanity and some totally unbelievable plots.'

'But he seemed so negative, bitter, dark.'

'Patrick sensed the goodness in people and so he explored their corresponding darkness, which is, you must admit, more visible. He believed in the elemental continuity of the human soul, the dynamic complementarity of our mental states. His characters do not aim to become heroes – or anti-heroes. They are not very intelligent, either. They act in the mists of semi-awareness of what they are doing. I think Patrick did the same. He was not always sure of his work. As a matter of fact, he was *never* certain about it, so he left his stories with meaningful gaps and suggestive missing links. He never wanted to punish his readers with truths that left no space to breathe.'

Here he paused.

'I repeat: he didn't victimize his readers, as Tolstoy and Dostoevsky did, and to a certain degree, Conrad and Lawrence also, by loading on to them the burden of an unimaginable destiny, or by revealing to them great truths with nothing to do with their lives. Great truths, as you may already know, are easily forgotten. He treated his characters with respect even when he depicted them as evil. Evil is always charming; it has so many followers. They are untested by tragedy, so the see the aesthetics of pain not its sharpness. I admired Patrick's inconsistencies: the Greek word for admiration – isn't it great?–*thaumasmos!* Meaning simultaneously miracle, wonderment, awe, bewilderment and estrangement? What a word!'

'Yes, it is a very beautiful word.'

'Not simply beautiful, but accurate.'

'An unexpected bombardment of lapidary statements. You seem to know so many things,' I said in awe.

'It is because of my solitude,' he replied. 'Solitude helps you listen to the slightest sound with respect. Yet we all know that until the last day we must fight against our inner demons, which unfortunately are the best part of ourselves. Or maybe fortunately? What makes us human is our urge to explore our bestial nature. When the spirit emerges in us, or comes into us, it is really too late. We have already been seduced by those demons, and the only gift we can offer is tears. Very insubstantial offer indeed. You cannot receive the spirit without having surrendered to the demons first: they are our entrance ticket.'

He pronounced the word *pneuma* by stretching his voice as if he were caressing it with his lips.

'What prevails in the end is penitential compunction – that's all. We end up inarticulate and confused. It's sad, really. There is a kind of goodness which is really malevolence. By striving to be good, we simply destroy the ambivalence of life, together with, along the way, some gullible people.'

Another deep Greek word: *enantiodromia.* Heraclitus. Its exact translation is 'opposing trajectories'. Did he ever read the dark philosopher?

'And, if I may add to this: there is a kind a badness which is beneficial. It makes your will obsolete and then you begin to think. Probably something changes in us when we feel helpless. But I feel that I have lost my argument here.'

He stopped. He looked at me as if surprised I was still there. He shook his head and murmured something which I couldn't hear. You had the impression that he was trying to touch something invisible hovering over both of us.

Some time later he gave a very touching interview on television.

My friend Sybille Smith said: 'He weighed his words one by one with the precision one uses in a second language.'

His Greek was so vast and magnificent that every discussion threw me into deep despair.

'You have so much to learn,' he told me with sympathy.

'Mr Lascaris, I have just been promoted to Senior Lecturer,' I protested.

'Some institutions are victims of their own regulations, young man,' he said, shaking his head sceptically.

I couldn't deny that, even if it involved me.

Sanity

'I am not a literary critic, *buuuut–*' That prolonged *buuuut* was his battle cry. I asked him once about the books he liked reading.

'The classics,' he said, without hesitation. 'The Greek classics, of course. The Latin writers have something derivative, something puerile, as if they were trying to establish an identity for themselves. Then Shakespeare, Tolstoy, and as we have discussed many times before, Chekhov, my real love. I can't say anything about Patrick's books because I will be incriminated. Any more questions?'

Given the opportunity, I dared to proceed.

'What makes a good writer?'

'Sanity,' he immediately replied. 'Not style, nor art, nor plot, but sanity of vision.'

'How do you mean?' I asked.

'Sanity is the ultimate tragic condition of being, an incurable mental disease. The sane mind is forced to create imaginative forms in order to alleviate its unfortunate situation.'

'With due respect, Tolstoy was the ultimate nutcase,' I said, using an improper Greek colloquialism to describe the great man.

'Hold your tongue, young man.' He was agitated. 'Tolstoy was the only writer who dealt with human frailty as something deeply metaphysical. That's sanity: to see the ultimate truth in mortality.'

'Mr Lascaris,' I dared to say, 'that is so Christian, so monkish!'

'You are very perceptive when you want to be,' he grinned. 'But don't forget that it can also be Stoic or even Buddhist. *Buuuut* obviously you misunderstood my statement: sanity is not something good or positive. A writer must transform sanity into an advantage, because being sane today means to be peripheral. Patrick struggled to make his sanity an advantage for his writing. Remember the deranged world of *The Aunt's Story?* And look at the serene, detached, ironic voice of his last works. Irony means love, young man. He deeply loved everything he denounced in his novels. I insist: you must see his works as immense parodies, especially his last works, which are parodies of his own style.'

'It's funny, Mr Lascaris,' I said, 'but that's exactly my understanding of *The Vivisector,* for example, which I have been translating for years.'

'Spot on!' he exclaimed triumphantly. 'Many critics haven't understood what a civilized writer Patrick was. He could be ironic or even dismissive towards his own achievements. How many writers can do that? They all take themselves so seriously that they become laughable.'

He was on fire.

'Yes, I know, on many occasions modesty can be the most shameless pretence. Well, you know, that's what Patrick totally lacks: pretence. When he talks to you, he is not elsewhere. He is *in* everything he says: in the language, in the ideas, in the presentation. You don't have that impression with Tolstoy, for example. He wanted to be a priest but was forced to have twelve children. Even in his best moments, you feel a second Tolstoy grinning beneath the pages. Tolstoy the preacher, Tolstoy the reformer, Tolstoy the Messiah. Patrick is like Plato: he strikes with the astounding clarity of devastating truths. He exposes you to danger, which is not very pleasant.'

'Some critics have accused his language of being pretentious and artificial,' I whispered.

He moved his hands up and down against an invasion of invisible elephants. Then he recovered his composure and continued majestically:

'Some writers create out of self-pity, out of lack and loss. Patrick never did. He wrote out of the fullness of being in our common space. He didn't write out of the fear of death, or the artificial paradise of a lost youth. I insist: he wrote because our common space gave him sufficient gravity to remain constantly attached to this earth. He was never motivated by illusions. He never experienced a crisis in our common space. And he never wrote obscenities, even in his most complex work such as *The Eye of the Storm,* or his most confusing like *The Twyborn Affair*. He never talked about sex and penises and orgies. That would have been so low-class! We both agreed we would have none of that.'

He used a very ancient Greek word for the male member. In the beginning I didn't understand; he had to explain it to me in more modern vulgar Greek.

'This is the Hippocratic word for the male anatomy,' he added loftily.

'Well, Mr Lascaris,' I said, 'I have never heard that term before.'

'Irrelevant,' he said raising his hand towards my face, commanding me to shut up. 'Any story must say a lot about the human body; if not, it must talk about its clothes. It must clothe the body with whatever will show its plasticity and beauty. That's what Patrick did in most of his novels. The fabric of clothes indicates the hidden secret of his characters. He avoided any form of style: style is self-defence. Indeed, he divested himself of all style in his last work, where he reached the ultimate self-revelation. He became himself; he didn't pretend. He was simply himself. That was both relief and redemption. I was there; I saw it all happening. Along the way we listened to a lot of music together. That was enough to keep us close.'

Our discussion had circled back to him. This was my golden opportunity to ask about their intimate relationship, I thought. In response, an outburst of strange words in Greek, English, and French assaulted my ears. Finally something lucid came out.

'Curiosity? Morbid curiosity you mean,' he said. 'That's sickening, Mr Vrasidas – that's sickening.'

'I'm sorry,' I said in shame. 'I must go now. I have kept you far too long.'

He came with me to the door. A sudden storm over Sydney had made everything dark. As I was waiting for a taxi on the doorstep, he touched my shoulder with his right hand and started talking, as if from a parallel universe.

'Listen, if you are interested in Patrick's work you should know that his books are superior to his existence, even to our life together. They depicted a world which is stronger and heavier than my self and his self. So they cannot be reduced to particulars of his life. The books are good because they were inevitable. Don't ask for any personal information, because even if I tell you, you can't draw any conclusions from it. Modern literature is a profitable trade of dreams, fantasies, hallucinations. His work is beyond these tricks. Don't forget: anything that can be represented or photographed is already sanitized or domesticated.'

The rain was pouring over the Park.

'Patrick wanted to work with the anarchy and the bestiality of the heart. He wrote about the unwritability of life; what you find in his novels is the complaint of the writer at the limitations of his craft. Think about this without falling in with the James Joyce cult. Joyce, after his first works and the first chapters of *Ulysses,* vanished as a writer, because he thought that the writing was everything. Patrick struck a balance between Joyce and Proust. He created something unique because while he was writing, there was a very great deal of it which remained unsaid. And therein lies the creative synergy between writer and reader.'

It was raining; I was bursting; I wanted to go home – but I wished that he would never end this brief course on writing. Oh yes, he was a great teacher – without students. And more: his imperial ancestry occasionally emerged as the misplaced commandments of a General.

'I have never accomplished anything,' he said with an ambiguous smile, 'but I will die having exhausted my creativity.'

'Thank you, I said, with sincere gratitude. I was still bursting.

'That is so sentimental,' he laughed.

Behind us was that metaphysical house, sober and sullen. It was the darkness, the rain, the urgency to go, that together gave me an impression of diabolical laughter.

The Italian cab-driver told me: 'That man look *molto mysterioso ...* is he aristocratic?'

'Drive fast,' I shouted. 'I'm bursting–'

'Mate, don't piss in my cab, awright?'

Mr Lascaris never let me use his toilet, something which puzzled and tortured me a lot. Or didn't I ever dare ask?

Furniture

It was a humid October evening, smooth and liquid. We went to our usual restaurant in the Park. We ordered fish and chips and drank water.

'Not even Coke? I asked him.

'No, no – bad for your stomach.'

Paternal feelings, I thought.

Unexpectedly, he started talking about furniture, which in the beginning I found odd and confusing.

'Essentially furniture refers to our relationship with space,' he said, pointing his finger an inch in front of my eyes. 'Our home is defined by our movements around spaces vital to our lives. Beds, tables, chairs, sofas – anything of this sort – determine our daily self-definition. We remake ourselves every day according to the position of objects, as we move in between them. So they must be intimate and personal. Avoid symbols in your private sphere! They spoil all intimacy. When furniture changes, you change. When they fade with time, you change too, because the way you see them changes. And movement, as you know, implies navigation.'

He used the Greek word *periplous,* meaning circumnavigation, which I hadn't heard for years.

'Talking about our furniture,' he continued, 'gives you the rare opportunity to understand my own form of existence. Maybe this is too religious for you?'

'Oh, no, no,' I said. 'What then is the essential being of things?'

'You don't understand Patrick's novels!' he shouted. 'That's so bad!' There was contempt all over his face. '"Essential being"? We don't sell such ideas here, sir! We are decent people. We excel in the prosaic virtues of living!'

His voice was loud, agitated and dismissive.

My public humiliation was attracting attention. He continued his attack.

'Furniture creates the space in which our senses become actual. We live through furniture. That's more than enough, no? Do we need anything else? No! We are made of the space that surrounds us.'

At Martin Road, he lived surrounded by the colours of the late 1960s and early 70s: bright green, yellow, orange and red, faded but nevertheless still gaudy. He never let me go up into his bedroom to see the greys, blacks and the browns that dominated the upper space. It was years later when I was offered a fleeting glimpse of that hidden domain, when he showed me a painting over Patrick's writing desk.

'I will never forget the day these colours came into our lives,' he said now. 'Can you remember when you first saw those colours? By looking at them, new emotions can enrich your mind.'

'Mr Lascaris,' I said, 'this is Goethe's theory of colour.'

'Well, so what? I grew up with him. Goethe is a matter of class. Can't you see how important colours are for the understanding of reality?'

I needed time to think.

'Patrick's writing desk gives me a more accurate record of the time than the clock, because of the way its timber creaks,' he said.

I thought he was teasing me with metaphysical speculation. After all, I had told him about my involvement with Theosophy.

He helped himself to all the sauce tartare to eat with his fish.

'Would you like some tomato sauce?' he asked.

'We don't eat fish and chips with ketchup,' it was my turn to say.

'But look at its colour,' he said softly, as if caressing the words. 'Like the brightness of fresh blood.'

I felt this was enough for that day. As we were walking back, he started talking to himself, although I was next to him.

'Patrick wrote out of sadness – yes, it was sadness. He wrote with sadness, not for his life, his family or his country. No – he had met certain people who made him deeply sad. Sadness, as you know, leads to compunction and contrition – that's it! Yes, some people made him sad and led him to opening his heart. Sometimes I wonder if I was not one of them. Who knows? He's dead now, so we will never get to the truth. Anyway, he couldn't reconcile himself with life after that sadness. The thread that connects all his work is, I think, the question of how people perpetuate their misunderstandings of one another. All his work is about misunderstanding. Like *The Vivisector,* a novel for those who hate easy solutions. *The Vivisector,* the story of those who understand that futility is the mother of creative impulse. Only when you understand how futile everything is, do you want to save anything. And then you inexorably fail. We save something when we fail to save it. Paradoxical, no? Tricky also! Painful too.'

This must be one of his soliloquies, I thought.

'Have you seen a man crying and his body shaken by spasms of agony? I held Patrick's body in such a state, in my arms. After that you have a completely different understanding of life. You feel that you have been sanctified; you don't have to say anything, because your life through its silence will say something beyond words. I love words for what they can do – but things existed before their intervention. Judging people from the results of their actions is definitely useful, but understanding their motives is really divine. He wrote out of sadness because people never tried to understand his intentions. They insisted on his failures, which were very obvious; he was the first to know them. Sadness makes people noble in the Greek sense of the word: *of good nature.* It essentially makes their natures pure. How should I say it? His purity generated my silence – and that made me happy. Happiness, of course, doesn't mean much; we're not here to be happy. Let's say he made me complete by showing me the end. After sadness come contrition and compunction, the triptych that fulfils existence.'

In front of their house he turned to me. He was surprised, I thought, that I was still there.

'The other thing you have to remember about Patrick is his solitude. He was lonely, somehow friendless, unable to communicate.'

'I have read about his notorious temper and his falling out with so many people,' I said.

'Gross exaggerations! He had the exact measure for everybody around him. He sensed why people were befriending him and the reasons they used his name.'

'Fair enough,' I said, 'but was he able to relate to other people? Was he able to understand the other?'

'Honestly speaking, no. Any other person was an enigma to him; he struggled to understand it but became further puzzled, frustrated and angered by their contradictions. Later in his life this became his fascination, but earlier it was just frustration. Different names for the same situation, I think.'

'Well then,' I took the liberty, 'did he ever understand you?'

He replied as if I was not even there. He spoke without stopping, as if he wanted to get everything out in one asthmatic breath, as if he needed to drive out something buried deeply in his mind.

'His last will and testament show that he didn't. But our shared life illustrated his constant desire to give me a home within the boundaries of his life. I was his frustration and his inspiration, his confusion and his serenity, his character and his nothingness. I lost myself as he was trying to discover me. I got tired, and in my fatigue he saw an omen. I lost hope, and in my despair he found encouragement. I felt abandoned, and in my resignation he found repose. It was very unpredictable. He was trying to find somebody in the wrong place, while constantly having him in front of his eyes! I suppose we must represent the adventure of many couples who try to find their partner somewhere else than in their mortal bodies. I dreamed of leaving him and moving back over the blue waves of our sea, but it was only a dream. His hands brought me back to reality. They were soft, white, supple, the hands of a Renaissance Platonist drawing allegories in the cave.'

Suddenly he looked intensely at me.

'Are you still here?' he asked, amazed.

He had forgotten all about me. Yet his monologue was beautiful and dramatic. He moved his hands in the air as if he were trying to write his real life down on invisible paper, inscribe what he had locked in his mind for so long.

'Mr Lascaris,' I dared, 'how did you manage to keep your thoughts secret for so long? Did you talk with anyone?'

He glared at me and said abruptly:

'These secrets belong to me and to him, to the moments of our shared encounters. Nothing to do with you and your morbid curiosity.'

I didn't have time to reply. We had reached the house, and he rushed inside and slammed the door. I could hear sounds from behind it. Was he crying or was it the rustling of the leaves under my feet that made me shiver?

Friendship

I never understood why he didn't like bringing his friends together.

'Tomorrow, David will be here. And the day after, Kate. And then Barbara. Next week the other David, and then Robert.' And what about that shadowy 'Jim'? He never asked me to come along and join them. I was desperate to meet David Marr, whose biography had become in my mind a model of insight. But this was not to happen.

'We must keep these meetings purely Greek,' Mr Lascaris told me, when I dared to raise the possibility.

'After I am gone, you will meet David, who is a real gentleman. You are very impetuous and impatient. I think that you won't like one another. He is very refined and sophisticated, whereas you are a bit rough around the edges – very proletarian.'

At that moment a tall gentleman appeared with his dog at the door. After restrained greetings, they started talking about the British royal family: about the Queen and Diana and Charles and Phil the Greek, together with some of the other names which in their absolute ordinariness belong to the royal families of Europe. They even reached back to the last Richard who had sat on the English throne, and explained why no other Richard had been crowned since. Riveting stuff!

The gentleman left after they had exhausted all the latest gossip about the reigning couple, so brutally disparaged by White in *Flaws in the Glass.*

'I sense,' he said, 'that you didn't really understand what all that was about.'

'Mr Lascaris,' I replied, 'there were only republicans in my family. My grandfather was twice thrown into prison for no reason whatsoever by the family of that moronic Phil of yours. Sorry – I can't understand all that.'

'It's a matter of family origins,' he said dismissively, a strange cruel expression on his face.

Trying to ignore this, I asked him: 'Mr Lascaris, do you ever feel nostalgia for your childhood?'

He looked stunned by my question; it took him some time to think. He hummed for a long time, biting his lips and moving his tongue over them.

'I don't want to be indiscreet,' I added. 'but as an expatriate myself, I would like to know what happens after you live for so long in another country.'

He gazed at me with compassion.

'Well, as the ancients used to say: *omnia mea mecum porto,* my home is my body. I have no other beginning or end. So wherever my body is, my home is also built. Memory? I know that's a bit tricky. Memory is a trap. As you start talking about the past, language absorbs you – I mean the language of your early years. As you know, in my childhood I spoke three languages. Greek was the most immediate and social, but English and French were within my grasp too, plus occasional German. Goethe, you know – an appropriate writer for my class, as I've already told you. Later we must not forget the mighty Arabic language, in Alexandria. Haunting guttural sounds, as if subterranean gods were trying to make contact with us. So in a sense I was always divided. Yet I must admit that Greek is the language I can clearly hear in my dreams. My heart leaps when I hear it around me. When my sister last visited Australia and we went to Queensland, I felt so strong and joyful. Her Greek made me so self-sufficient, so full within myself. But here I am; I have spent most of my life in a new land, being to a certain degree afraid to get in touch with other Greeks. You know, some of them are horribly prejudiced. *Buuuut* I must tell you: I never felt a foreigner in this country. No, never, no! And this had nothing to do with Patrick. It's the country itself: she invites you to inhabit her. To such a call you must respond, otherwise you lose your self and your good manners. My upbringing never allowed me to decline a well-meant invitation. Australia *is* an open invitation, promising, gentle, indirect. Nothing in excess here. The classical sense of proportion and balance became reality here, not in Europe.'

Outside his house, I heard the aggressive territorial cry of a kookaburra. The weather had started changing. We were talking about nostalgia and memory. The kookaburra interfered with our voices. We stopped and listened to the loud interruptions of the uninvited guest.

'Nature is always against the civilizing process of human conversation,' he said.

And: 'It is so hard to accept that your country of origin is not your true motherland.'

The weather

'The only real inhabitant of Sydney is its weather. Our human adventures in the city reflect prevailing conditions. We follow the weather's unpredictability and indifference. I always feel that we live at the mercy of its patterns in this country. Not many people have paid attention to this, but we immigrants immediately spot the subtle gradations of colours in the clouds that make the real difference in our day-to-day life. And we are more sensitive to human moods, so we immediately perceive changes in the weather.'

'Mr Lascaris,' I said, 'this sounds like Osho's cloud metaphysics. That was a very singular observation for a Voltairian spirit like yours.'

'Your wit is extremely poor,' he grinned. 'For us, the weather has always been a natural chorus in the background of our private stories.'

'Who are *us?*'

'Patrick and I,' he said. 'Haven't you noticed the ways the weather is depicted in his novels? If you study the differences between his first three works and the later ones, you will see that his great novels are essentially *about* the weather. From *The Tree of Man* to *The Eye of the Storm,* Patrick was extremely cautious about talking about the weather and representing its presence. He acted like those Sufi sages who wrote treatises about love without ever referring to it.'

I interrupted him impatiently. 'Do you mean that his early novels were mystical tracts?'

He clasped his hands in frustration, exasperation, vexation.

'What can I say that you won't misconstrue?' he asked. 'As time went by, Patrick's writing became subtler. It depicted a story *in statu nascendi.* That was my influence: as we grow older and our body disintegrates, we understand the process of birth. I alerted him to the changing patterns of the weather so that he could see the influence of those invisible, omnipotent natural elements on human life. He was very grateful, because reality cannot be convincingly represented if you ignore the obvious. We never see it; that's our problem. And when we *do* see it, we don't like it. It is really sad that today's writers prefer hallucinations and illusions. But we went beyond that: we have seen the visible, with heart-breaking lucidity. If this is mysticism, so be it. To my mind, however, it is simple brightness. Only then are minds, objects and situations able to be deciphered, when they can be seen through and through. In Greek, *diaphaneia:* what a word! The more you see, the more you are: this is the consolation of our senses!'

He shook his head.

'It is so sad that you cannot also see the visible,' he added. His voice was full of disappointment. 'You know, this is the reason you can't have abstract thoughts. Because you underestimate the concrete and the specific. Only when you see the distinct nature of every object does your mind struggle to establish connections between them, and consequently you realize the importance of abstraction. I am talking elementary Aristotle here. You most obviously ignore his work!'

'I have to work on this,' I said to myself. Yet I was not allowed to comment or even breathe.

'Don't try to respond,' he ordered. 'You will just expose your ignorance again.'

It started raining.

'See – our conversations follow the patterns of the weather,' he concluded, an expression of victory on his face.

As usual, the Greeks have a word for this: *cyclothymia,* used by psychiatrists to designate moodiness and dejection.

Another dream

'I was thrown into a deep cave. I couldn't find a way out. Then there was a breeze, rasping over me: *Do not be afraid.* I heard that voice with my skin. It was the voice of my mother. The cave was dark, humid, mythic, and I felt the crackling of cockroaches crushed under my feet.'

He paused, then continued. 'Old age made me sensitive to dreams. I can't remember the things I have to do every day, but I always remember my dreams. How do you explain that? You say you have studied psychoanalysis.'

'I tried, Mr Lascaris, but I failed. Too much cruelty in the profession. Yet I do know that dreams happen when the synapses in the brain loosen. This happens when we are asleep, but I also know of many people who dream when they are not asleep.'

'I know some too,' he said, bending his head and holding it with both hands. 'The day-dreamers, the somnambulists who cause so much havoc–'

He didn't get my point.

'Mr Lascaris,' I interrupted him, 'day-dreamers are idealists and all idealists are afraid of order.'

'You are right!' he exclaimed triumphantly, as if something quite unexpected had come out of my mouth.

'Anarchy is always creative, no?' he asked. 'I have read a bit of Scott Fitzgerald and still remember his sentence: *All life is a process of breaking down.* Isn't that a great line? He is a very sweet writer, despite the fact that he managed to make a whole empire seem provinicial – not a small achievement, by any standards. True: we gradually break down from the unity of childhood, a unity, mind you, due to lack of conscience. At the moment we start understanding where we are, the process of disintegration begins. Dreams make that process obvious and poignant.'

He paused and breathed heavily.

'Now he will say something bad about me,' I thought. But he didn't. He revisited his dream.

'Can you imagine my mother whispering over me in a cave? I can't remember ever having *been* in a cave. I must confide in you, young man, the ultimate fruit of my contemplation: imagination perfects experience. Experience unmakes our world; imagination puts it back together, reassembles it. Patrick said: *Only those with imagination can discover reality.* Isn't that great? My imagination completes and perfects my experience; it helps us to realize our potential.'

'You have a deep reverence towards the real, I see, Mr Lascaris,' I dared. 'Yet you are not a realist. As I understand it, you are an idealist without idealization.'

'I love reality too much to be a realist, in exactly the same way that as a humanist I must admit that "humanity" is grossly over-estimated. I take things as they come. We need some form of idealism – at least *I* need it. But I don't reduce anything to Platonic ideas. I construct no idols. I don't even see the sacred in all these. The sacred is what we can never love. Do you understand? You can't love what cancels you out, what overpowers you. I believe in the horizontal dimension. The amorphous substance of life in general is beyond my feelings. Subtle innuendos make the real difference; from them we have to reconstruct life from the perspective of the unfulfilled.'

'What about love, Mr Lascaris? Can it help? How does it work in us?'

'I like your question; you are improving,' he said with satisfaction. 'There is only one way to describe the in-between situation in which you find yourself when you love. It goes back to Sappho: *bitter-sweet eros* (Γλυκύπικρoςέρως), so between, so mixed, so impure. We are all impure. Our act of loving purifies us, but it has to be done with lots of sweat and detergent. Somebody must wash the clothes and look after the sick. *Bitter-sweet:* such a beautiful word in Sappho's lonely verse.'

'I didn't know that you read poetry, Mr Lascaris.'

'You are a very sad case of a presumptuous proletarian, young man! Poetry is my real breathing space,' he added, exasperated.

I knew then that it was time for me to go. Since my early youth I had encountered teachers who had humiliated me so much that in the end I took perverse delight in it. Now I could easily take more.

But he yawned and said:

'I have another dream to tell you – but maybe some other time.'

That's what he was: the man of may or may-not. I felt so satisfied that I had finally been able to pin him down with such an elegant and memorable sentence.

'It's a very interesting dream,' he continued. 'Come back soon.'

I was kicked out of his house. Yet still I felt immense satisfaction. Why?

God

It was the 25 July 1995. I remember this because of the inevitable phone call from my mother on my birthday. Mr Lascaris was suffocating inside his house, so we decided to take a stroll. Soft evening, haunted silence. The legendary stillness of the trees.

'Mr Lascaris, we are like Boswell and Johnson!' I announced with joy.

'What are you planning for the future?' he asked. 'Please do not write anything. I want my soul to maintain its innocence – and you are so corroded by suspicion. For you writing must be some kind of black magic.'

I remained silent.

The sun was still bright. Clouds could be seen over the horizon. That evening he talked about God or 'the name that names its absence', as he put it.

'Is this some sort of negative theology, Mr Lascaris?' I asked.

'Oh, no, no,' he replied. 'I remember a tense discussion I had with Patrick, out there in Castle Hill so many years ago. Probably the years themselves have given that name an existence that then we cannot see. Certainly his death transformed our discussion. It is important to understand what life is or even if there is such a thing as life, in order to understand that name.'

'I think we are becoming too sceptical,' I said. 'How can we refute our presence here? Do we need a reference to something that is *not* here?'

'I must tell you a dream,' he said, 'which I had when I was digging the ground and looking after the dogs at Castle Hill. I was on the earth in prehistoric times. People were still building their own shelters. But soon the places they lived were gradually inhabited by fears, shadows and suspicions. The very act of living in them transformed their spaces into living entities. In every corner there was a shadow, in every dark spot some terrible dark presence, under the sleeping places sinister smiles without faces. These entities became so real that they were no longer afraid of the light. They moved around in every house without shame or guilt, unconcerned at the havoc they were causing. People started believing that each dwelling could not be inhabited as long as their builders lived in them. So they decided to exchange them, to share the fears and suspicions that were not theirs, so didn't really matter to them. The "conversion moment", as it came to be called, was so painful that people decided to detach themselves completely from the process of building. They created a special occupation, special life training for a group of people they called mediators. They were responsible for the building of dwellings so that no personal entities would be ever created by those who made them. A voice then told me: "The relation between people and their home is called God." *Theos* in Greek means the permeator. I heard it from an inner voice which I could see – I repeat I could *see* the voice in my own dream.'

'That's very Oriental, Mr Lascaris,' I said. 'Very African, to be precise.'

'Obviously we can't see below the surface,' he said impatiently. 'The Greeks have a word for you: *epidermic.*'

'I know that,' I said calmly. 'But the fundamental question is simple: does God exist? According to my understanding, you do what Plato and Jesus did before you: you replace the question with an elegant formulation. You employ myths, parables, stories to depict what you call "God". By telling the story, you create the experience; hence "God" becomes real.'

He took a deep breath, and seemingly in despair, he replied:

'Straight answer to your fundamental question: God does not normally exist, but when we build houses, create forms or invent stories, he exists.'

I persisted.

'This is again vague and metaphoric, Mr Lascaris. It is very elusive. How can we say that God exists only when we build houses and the rest?'

His reply came with a devastating smile.

'Building a house means building a relationship. Our relationships are God's epiphanies or – to be precise – they bring God to life. The same can be said about artistic forms and stories. Everything that re-creates the existing is God.'

He stopped and then added.

'Of course, I understand your disbelief. I feel equally frustrated by all these superficially religious people who always put God at the beginning of everything. I see God at the end, as the conclusion, as the ultimate reality after the transience of the organic. Yet we have to live the organic in all its corruptibility and lack of meaning in order to experience the inorganic. Before, there is no *is.* After, there is *it.* It has emerged as meaning through lives lived and stories experienced, remembered, recollected. The image and likeness is not an essential given: it is what we must do and become. It is a destination, not a destiny.'

'Mr Lascaris,' I mumbled. 'this is so ... so ... so ... Hellenic. So natural theology. So unbelievable!'

'Healthy scepticism,' he said, with his disarming smile. 'But you need a personal catastrophe in order to look for that wordless inorganic something beyond your existence. Only when you fall into disorder do you feel the need for the inorganic plenitude of personal death.'

This was incomprehensible, unacceptable, totally unmeaning.

'Your mind is demonically possessed by adjectives!' he laughed.

How did he understand that?

'But listen carefully, he added, with compassion, 'it is our psyche that resists words, not God. When you understand how inarticulate we really are about the things we care for most, then you will feel the bare bones of your consciousness as an immediate presence.'

'Mr Lascaris,' I complained, 'I must express my own truths in the way that I find most appropriate.'

This was really epidermic.

'You don't possess any truths to express,' he said, full of despair and ... and ... and ... benevolence. 'It will happen eventually, but only when you understand that having been so lucky has deprived you from discovering the real. As I told you earlier, you force me to commit the dreadful sin of repetition. Building a home means building a relationship! Keep this in mind and even if you fail to do it, you will be on the right path.'

It was late, and I had to go. Too many cryptic pronouncements for a single day.

But when I went home, I couldn't sleep. I thought that this clumsy parable was really interesting, even if his ideas were irritating. The next day I called him early in the morning and asked if I could see him at noon.

'Very impatient today, Mr Vrasidas,' he said with irony in his voice. 'Are you tormented again by the shadows of your past?'

As far as I recall I had never talked to him about myself. I ignored the remark.

'Can I be there at one?'

'OK.'

I arrived gasping, with a question in my mouth.

'If we return to our discussion of yesterday, what about the homeless people, Mr. Lascaris? I mean metaphorically and literally.'

'Homelessness is our only reality,' he replied, almost annoyed. 'But our mental life emerges in that paradox of building our home against the shifting sands of homelessness. This is adequately discussed in *The Eye of the Storm,* which I recommend you read so that you won't ask me such questions again.'

After a brief silence he sighed, and said:

'You are lost in your quest for doctrines, truths and theologies. I am afraid that you see religions as social assets or cultural decoration, as most people do. I see them as substitutes and epiphenomena of our inability to imagine or live holiness. And you know what? You don't realize the importance of original sin. That's why you're so keen on finding truths. Only when you understand what original sin is will you be able to discover what life is about.'

'And what is the meaning of original sin?' I asked, full of curiosity.

'Original sin is the first mistake committed at the time humanity was born. Isn't the Greek term *the forefather's failure* more appropriate to express the condition of being bound by history? Isn't it true that this failure has nothing to do with nature, even human nature, but with history, with human actions? Very few people notice this – with the exception of certain Jewish thinkers, of course. They are the most history-making nation of the earth.'

'This is so heretical, Mr Lascaris!' I whispered.

He laughed. Suddenly he put his hand into the right pocket of his cardigan, and brought out a bar of Greek chocolate. He broke it in half.

'Have some,' he said. 'It will make you feel better. I shouldn't be eating it, but you know, how can I resist the taste of Greek chocolate?'

He was making fun of me again.

'Well,' he continued through the piece of chocolate in his mouth, 'my heretical idea is simple: we must re-live that initial failure in order to discover history. Very few nations have the strength to do it – and very few individuals, too. They take cover beneath institutions and habits, like churches and families, and these make them forget the need for redemption. So death becomes the only way out. Please read *The Eye of the Storm;* it is precisely about this!'

I had in fact just started reading the novel, which I was finding too morbid, too reminiscent of my own horrible family. He added:

'Well, since you have this obsession with God, I will say something that will confuse you even further: even if God exists, all thinking and sensitive humans, and artists in particular, must preach atheism. Their negation will give a new lease of life to our quest for relationships. On the other hand, everybody talks, so the silence of God is what makes action possible. On this I will have to refer you to *Riders in the Chariot.* Just read it one day; it will make you understand what original sin, our forefather's failure, is about.'

Me obsessed with God? What about him?

He stopped for a moment, and then started laughing.

'But what am I talking about? I know nothing about such problems. Please ignore me. Only good chefs know the truth about God.'

I was irritated and confused.

Of a certain Greek writer

Memory can be so enigmatic, looking back to demolish the remnants of nostalgic illusion.

The 1950s were his first decade in the new country. The isolation of Castle Hill and the intensity of his relationship with Patrick were punctuated by visitors from the old homeland, reminding him of people and things idealized by the power of distance.

In 1956, an aspiring Greek writer, CT, arrived in Sydney, accompanied by a famous pianist as his pet boy. He lived in Sydney between 1956 and 1965, 'nine years of complete debauchery', as Lascaris would say with an expression of pity and contempt on his face. He always referred to CT using the feminine form. After several months, the pianist vanished to the United States, unable to cope with the sexual sybaritism.

'You can't imagine how much we suffered. Patrick avoided him with feelings of absolute disgust. Did you ever meet him?'

'We all knew him in Athens,' I replied. 'He was a very bad character. You know, of course, how he died?'

'No I don't,' he said. 'After he left Australia I never wanted to meet up with him ever again. Then back he came back in 1968 and tried to meet us. A totally uninhibited individual.'

'He was found strangled in 1988 in his own home,' I told him. 'He was dressed up in women's clothes. They had killed him in the early hours; it seems that throughout the night a whole army of concupiscent – if I may use the term in its Augustinian sense – soldiers paraded through his bed. He was drunk, drugged and did not resist. To this day, his assassin has not been found.'

'He remained faithful to his depravity to the last moment of his life!' he exclaimed pensively.

'Let's not be unfair, Mr Lascaris,' I dared. 'He was living out his passions. He was trying to express his real self.'

'You make me sound cruel and callous–*buuuut* this is what I am not. I respect each individual as much as he respects himself: no more, no less. When he was in Sydney, that man caused so much trouble–'

'I thought it would have been good for you, meeting another Greek in Sydney in the 50s, your first decade in you new country.'

'Just because we are Greeks it doesn't mean that we have to like or even befriend one another. He was a very rotten character, I'm telling you.'

'But what did he do? I don't know much about his stay in Sydney, except from what he mentions in his books.'

I was inflamed with curiosity.

'Let me tell you some of his exploits. He used to visit us once a month up at Castle Hill, or whenever we came to Sydney. I had to drive, since Patrick never learned. First he came on to Patrick with sexual intentions. Believe it or not, in front of me he grabbed his "apocryphal parts", as we say in Alexandria. Patrick was furious. The man was an insatiable nymphomaniac! And then, as if nothing had happened, he continued to visit us frequently and read to me in the most theatrical way a story he was writing in Greek in a form of long monologues by two or three women.'

'Two', I said.

'Well, two women of the lowest possible intelligence, of proletarian upbringing, speaking in vulgar language about the most sordid things. His idea of literature was writing about gossip in the laundry. He produced long tirades of ridiculous coarseness. No elevation, no soul-searching, nothing. Emptiness. Vacuity.'

'Oh yes, his most famous book, *The Third Wedding,* was partly written in Sydney,' I remembered. 'Actually, it is considered one of the best novels of post-War Greek literature.'

'That's why we don't have good writers in Greece, you know. Because they can't distinguish between what flatters your passions and what transforms them into literature.'

Unexpectedly, he used the immense Greek word *metousiosis,* a religious term from the Holy Communion.

'Let me finish his story. After so many meetings putting up with his boring monologues, I dared to tell him my humble opinion of what he said. I said it discreetly, understating my dislike. He jumped up in anger from the sofa on which he was reclining like a slothful empress, and yelled at me: "And what do you know about literature, you penniless, pompous silk stocking? You can't even get a good fuck!" He added something insulting about my "erotics" with Patrick which I dare not repeat to this day!'

'He was extremely vulgar – a real commoner,' I said. 'His only mission in life was to go round to any place where there was a wedding, and having the groom for himself – before the bride. He was extremely proud of such habits – and despite the fact that he was no Adonis, he claimed that no man ever denied him. He talked about such things on national television, with the innocence of an animal.'

'Now that says a lot about him – and his audience, no?' he commented in disgust.

'In one of his collections of short stories, he talks about the public toilets in Redfern and the anonymous pleasures he enjoyed there – for years. He practically lived in them,' I added, trying to bring on more revelations.

'I am never going to read them anyway,' he said like a stubborn child, and raised his hand in the gesture that meant he was telling me to shut up.

But I wanted more. I paused, remained silent for several minutes to add to the suspense, then said fast:

'In his autobiography he mentions how he tried to seduce his own father by rubbing his posterior against his genitals – when he was only seven years old!'

This would certainly add fuel to the fires of his moral indignation.

His face turned red. He got up from his chair and started walking up and down. He went into the kitchen and washed his hands. He opened the door to the little garden at the back. I was mystified, trying to detect the Freudian subtext of all this.

'His own father–' he muttered again and again.

'That's really Freudian!' I shouted triumphantly. But only to myself.

'Don't worry, Mr Lascaris: it was never consummated!' I elaborated sadistically. In fact CT never mentions anything at all like this in his heavily censored, posthumously-published memoirs. But I forged on:

'Three years later he seduced his uncle and his cousins, and started a spectacular career seducing all the male offspring of Adam! A friend of mine told me that during the German occupation he did a lot for the Resistance against the conquerors, keeping them busy night after night. At only fifteen he had whole regiments of Aryan animals at his sexual command. You know lonely men in a hostile land: they needed comfort.'

'Oh, noooo,' he shouted in despair and fury. 'Doing such abhorrent things with the conquerors of his motherland? While we were fighting against them in the desert! That's horrible! Most abominable!'

'But you must admit, Mr Lascaris,' I said, my sadism at its peak, 'that they were very sexy in their uniforms and boots. They were, alas, fighting with their bodies on completely misplaced battlefields!'

He became so angry that his hands shook. He avoided looking me in the eyes as he usually did. I thought that he was about to kick me out of the house. I rarely had the opportunity to provoke such strong reactions in him – and I must admit I was enjoying it. He was extremely agitated and annoyed, which gave me a feeling of minor victory. For the first time I had managed to elicit genuine reactions to the depths of his memories.

He gazed in despair at the icon of the Transfiguration, turned to me with disturbed shiny eyes and said:

'Literature, my friend, expresses our confrontation with evil. The stronger the evil we confront, the greater the literature we produce. The evil that exists is in us, surrounds us or is born through us, and exists because of us. Evil is the child of our delusions, the offspring of our obsessions. Using others for your own purposes is the beginning of all confusion. Literature encapsulates the words we whisper when we fight against the evil we embody. The intensity of our confrontation creates forms of transcendence: you transfer yourself one step beyond what you have confronted. Evil, the evil you have generated, is then objectified, and can be driven back. It is shown to be only a step forward, a stage of development.'

He stopped unexpectedly, looked around, and said:

'Of course, this happens only if you want to develop as an individual and are not arrested in some sort of Peter Pan syndrome of confusion. I am afraid our common friend suffered from that: he was terrified by the prospect of growing up. That can be seen in his books, from what you tell me, because Patrick's books, despite their disguised humour and masked playfulness, are books for adults. They are for people who have decided to grow up, and who have to deal with the problems of their souls. Of course this only happens if you *have* a soul and if you *want* to grow up. In the end it is a matter of aesthetics: being sixty years old and behaving as a young *trotteuse* is a real problem.'

'Mr Lascaris,' I dared, 'as I understand this, it is very moralistic. You sound almost Victorian. Why can't we let people live out their passions? That's what he was doing: he was being himself. Why should this prove so complicated?'

He smiled and then started laughing in a rather sarcastic manner.

'Reality is a great trap for those who don't know where they are. Their intensity remains unredeemed and their passions absorbed by the need for self-justification. They will never escape the pitfalls of becoming colourful exceptions.'

Back then, that was much too deep for me. I had started the discussion motivated by discovering some juicy gossip, and ended in moral reflection. I had to go.

'Mr Lascaris,' I said, 'I have kept you for far too long.'

'Yes, by all means,' he replied. Then he kept talking, on and on, about the CT affair – for three more hours. I didn't get home until ten in the evening.

The sound-proofing of buildings in Sydney is often not impressive. In the apartment next to mine a couple was drinking and screaming abuse at one another until early the following morning.

That was the only discussion I had with him about this commoner and his habits. The next time we met he didn't say anything about CT. It was as if he had never even been in Sydney.

Entropic memory devours the trivialities of our life. He finished with that single sentence: *Art expresses our confrontation with evil.* Isn't this a very existentialist remark from Patrick White's bedfellow?

Reading Australia

My usual anguish: I didn't know enough about Australia. I had read everything I could find: Manning Clark's dramatic, soul-consuming volumes. Mark Twain: irreverent. Anthony Trollope: solemn. Charles Darwin: frightening. And then D.H. Lawrence, *Kangaroo* and *The Boy from the Bush.* Bruce Chatwin's *The Songlines,* a magnetic stylistic achievement full of the elliptics of a mind plunged into sensual details. Strehlow's songs threw me into the abyss of time – lost, as always.

'*The Tree of Man?*' he asked.

Oops: I had forgotten it. 'I read it back in 1975 in a very bad Greek translation, and I don't think that I made any connection with it,' I said apologetically.

'Inexcusable,' he declared. 'If you want to know the essential Australia you must read it again and again. Despite its Australian theme, it is essentially a Russian story, which means it can happen anywhere. The ordinary nature of the story makes it exceptional. It's a story about space.'

'How do you mean?'

'Pay attention: space unlocks our senses. We can then open up to the complexities of the real. Strange words force our mind to make irrational claims on reality. Subtle innuendos make the difference. When we feel, nothingness is abolished. As St Paul would have said: *We are known by reality; we don't know it.'*

He used that strange word *tipote* in Greek, for nothingness. 'What-when' is the literal translation. Aristotle puzzled over its meaning.

'Why do we call nothingness "what-when" in Greek?' I asked.

'Because the ancient Greeks were pragmatists,' he responded, 'the way modern people aren't, despite their scientific mentality. They wanted to indicate that nothingness is the absence of space and time, which is in itself unimaginable. Can you imagine something which is nowhere? An old problem, of course. The only nothingness that exists is in our hearts, or the nothingness that we create through our inability to communicate. Nothing changes except our heart.'

'Mr Lascaris, last week you were telling me the opposite!'

'That's what I mean when I say that only our heart changes. It simply changes.'

I remembered my beloved verse: *I am large, I contain multitudes.* Whitman, so real and numinous, so alarming.

'But how can we trust each other if our discussions are full of contradictions?'

'Only people who are not logical enough see contradictions in antithetical statements. I see them as different stops along an uncharted itinerary. My presence defies all contradictions. Our discussions must be contradictory. Rational people are full of worries, so contradictions are the only way of expressing their experiences. Only the faithful have peace of mind – and they choose the language of paradox. The transition from the one to the other, from contradiction to paradox or the other way around, is probably the only proof we possess that we have a soul.'

Then suddenly he started talking about memories of Athens in the 1920s. Refugees in the streets, poverty, 'no milk anywhere', tuberculosis and dancing halls.

He wanted me to get out of his home. You didn't have to be a prophet to understand that.

The Thorn Birds

The phone rang. I had some visitors from Holland staying, in grief still for the death of a beloved friend in Amsterdam a year earlier. I didn't want to answer. The atmosphere was already heavy. I knew quite well that Dutch people never express their inner pain in case it is reported to the police.

'Go on!' Anton said. 'Pick up the phone! Eric is gone anyway; we can't bring him back. And your food is delicious.'

It was him. We hadn't talked for some time. He asked about my family in Greece:

'Are they all well? Did you visit my sister Elli? Did you see any good films?'

'Mr Lascaris, I said, 'I was in Greece last year. We have already talked about these things.'

'*These things* make your homeland,' he sighed. 'You should be more respectful.'

Then suddenly he picked up our conversation about novels from where we had left it several months before.

'My belief is that a novelist must slow down life. Patrick, as you might know, did so in *The Eye of the Storm:* seven hundred pages for a mother to die. Personally, I thought it was too short. Some mothers' dying could take thousands of pages. Patrick was over-generous. In novels, slow movement is the only kind, because it gives the reader time to be absorbed into the act of narrating. It also adds another dimension to the story; a novel is always about dialogue. The settings change, but what interests us is what people say about themselves to one another.'

Deep breath.

'Now, as you understand, dialogue is not always good. As a matter of fact, dialogue, as Plato knew all too well, is a dangerous way of delivering messages. It forces you to lose control over your story. Your interlocutors (our Greek word means co-researcher – isn't that great?) fragment your vision, especially when they think. Because many writers, especially Northern Europeans, make their characters think aloud. In Patrick's works they think as people *do* think, in silence. The ultimate outcome of every dialogue is sadness, because sadness is the final consequence of what cannot be achieved. Real dialogue would mean that people actually communicate. In fact, though we know that this has been the ideal of great visionaries, it has remained totally impossible throughout history.'

There was peculiar sorrow in his voice that made me feel awkward and somehow guilty.

'Mr Lascaris, with due respect, I have overseas visitors staying.'

A long pause and a sigh followed.

'I just wanted to help you with your research on Patrick.'

'Please,' I humbled myself, 'don't judge me over this. We're having dinner.'

'It will take me a long time to remember the rest,' he said. 'But I will call you again.'

Oh, no, no, noooo ... My only opportunity squandered for Dutch friends I don't really like anyway.

Politely he repeated: 'It always takes me time to remember.' And hung up.

I was punished. My visitors were shovelling up everything from their plates with complete satisfaction. I wanted to scream and cry.

One of them turned towards me with his mouth full, and mumbled:

'Have you discovered any good writers in Australia? There must be one good writer in this colonial outpost. Any names? We'll be flying to Perth tomorrow and I want some light reading for the flight. Five hours! As if we were flying to the centre of Africa.'

I told them that no, I hadn't discovered any good writers in Australia. They should read Colleen McCullough, who is universal.

'What a brilliant idea!' Anton exclaimed. '*The Thorn Birds* is a masterpiece. I saw the TV serial years ago, and I'll never forget it.'

Masculinity

It was a soothing, whistling, consenting day. We had decided to meet and wander around Centennial Park. A tourist came up and asked for directions to Bondi. Mr Lascaris was cheerful and animated. We walked for a long time and finally went to the restaurant at the centre of the Park for a late lunch.

'Allow me to pay,' he said. 'You look as if you have financial problems.'

I didn't know it was so obvious.

'Parents back home, Mr Lascaris,' I told him, 'asking constantly for money. They think that it comes easily in Australia. The sweet cruelty of emotional blackmail which we cannot escape. We succumb to its tyranny, painfully happy that we are doing our duty to our nearest and dearest.'

'Obviously you haven't grown up,' he said. 'You need to become a man, even in your 30s, if you want to become who you are. That's Pindar, of course. I think that the real name for this strange flow of images, events and emotions called life should be "help". Only by helping others can you become yourself.'

'I think that I understand what you mean,' I replied. 'But parents have their own hidden ways of keeping you an infant. It's like the morning news on television. They describe the most tragic events smiling with satisfaction so the viewers can see how happy they are that it did not happen to them.'

He paused.

'As you know, we did not possess such machines until Patrick's death. And I only infrequently watch it now. Very noisy! You simply have to grow up. Your generation is happy to remain infantile, the Peter Pan syndrome we talked about. But you deserve better. Think about us: forced to abandon paternal protection, maternal warmth, fraternal solidarity. Totally uprooted, we had to imagine our own destiny. Through our imagination we gained our manhood, in the most biological sense of the word.'

'I can't follow you, Mr Lascaris,' I whispered.

He laughed with compassion.

'Let me rephrase this: someone else makes you into a man. You can't do it yourself, even if your body grows. You simply have to find that person. Otherwise you remain in that limbo of maybes, the endless narthex before the altar, in the blissful confusion of childhood and adolescence. *Buuuut* do not forget: our childhood is pre-historic. We cannot become historical when our mind remains in our childhood.'

'I know what you mean,' I consented, defeated.

'As an observation of a cultural nature, you must have noticed that Anglo-Saxons worship childhood, whereas

Mediterraneans live fixated on their adolescence. Big difference, don't you think?'

'Oh, yes,' I replied. 'It is because they are the first to lose their childhood. Mediterraneans love confusion.'

'Do not judge!' he commanded, responding to my irony. 'As you age, you become more aware that all differences are matters of degree and emphasis, and humans simply fall victim to their inability to differentiate. I became a man because of Patrick. He forced me to discover my masculinity. Monogamy trans formed our shared life into something different: the Greek term would have been *oikopoeia,* home-making. Every room had our own scent, our own sinfulness. We treated love lightly and we made it last. I say that again: the axis of being is a sense of belonging. We belonged to each other, and that gave to our bodies a sacred feeling. Unconsciously, we made our lightness a matter for religious contemplation – and that was our *agape,* in the most theological sense of the word. We never felt like the notorious modern couples looking for cheap thrills in drugs, group orgies or anything else that makes them forget themselves. Modern couples hate themselves and avoid one another; each other represents what the other doesn't want to be, and so they create a completely false perception about "carnality" between men. You know what I mean: behaving like animals, using each other for pleasure without morality or consideration. What they call sex is the most obvious manifestation of self-hatred, malice and loathing.'

Sex? That was a very modern word for his vocabulary!

Suddenly the atmosphere became tense and ominous. Oh gods, make him talk more about this.

'It all comes down to ethics – unfortunately,' he continued, '*buuuut* don't you think that it would have been very ... very ... very ... *miserable* travelling around the planet, like Wilde, Gide, Genet and their like, in order to pick up "little musicians" who would become the turning points of their lives? How plebeian! They were unable to love and unable to expurgate the sin that makes us human through commitment. They had the naïve romantic idea that anything goes, and that after the death of God we are allowed to fall into the endless satisfaction of our urges. But I have to tell you something again and again: morality means the right moment to do something. And the only thing you can do in your life is to choose the life that will outlast you. That's morality.'

He ended triumphantly, then added:

'The most paradoxical thing in love is not that you love but that you have been loved, knowing all your deficiencies, your inner ugliness, the imperfections of your body. "How can anyone love *this?*" you wonder. *Buuuut* someone feels that *this* is good and beautiful! And the story begins: you enter his home and there is a plate on the table for you. You turn to your host with tears of gratitude. That's all. Eat now, because you make me forget my human nature with your lofty questions.'

Had I said anything? No. Had I asked anything? No!

Fish and chips had arrived on huge platters two hours after we had ordered.

'They are very slow in this place, Mr Lascaris,' I said.

'Are you in a hurry again?' he replied.

'No, no – nooo.'

'Well stay with me and enjoy the moment.'

A glass of white wine finally. Water for him.

'You scare me sometimes, Mr Lascaris,' I said shyly.

'I tend to have that effect on people who know nothing about life,' he said.

'Thank you,' I said, my ego totally demolished.

'Oh, no, no,' he protested, his hands scratching the air as if tearing hermetic nets apart. 'Don't take it personally! Remember again Pindar's life-saving verse which influenced Goethe: *epikrateivn duvnasqai (be able to control yourself),* and what I just said will take on its proper dimensions.'

'And what is the meaning of this verse?' I asked.

'Most men live in perpetual sexual exile. They search and search endlessly and aimlessly for sexual satisfaction that they will never attain, because they remain adolescents. The sexual desert of manhood blooms only through the body and the eyes of the person you love, in reciprocity; otherwise it becomes merely an exercise in self-justification.'

I felt that I couldn't swallow and was about to cry. Why?

The chips had stuck in my throat. Did he understand the *dysphoria* I was in?

'*Buuuut* I must remind you, my fellow Greek, of a very simple truth: the most important part of our house is its staircase – because it takes you in an upward direction. Isn't it the same with the word *anthropos* in Greek? Doesn't it mean upward-tending? If what you are doing does not lead you to the vertical dimension, then it is like these chips. They are stuck in your throat because they are oily and burnt; they cause discomfort, which you then project on to me, thinking that I don't care for your misadventure. This is what you like to think. Truth is always cruel, no?'

'You must be a mind-reader, Mr Lascaris,' I spluttered, coughing and trying to spit out the nasty burnt chip.

'Some people turn narcissistic out of low self-esteem,' he added. I couldn't see the connection with the current situation. 'Deep down, you yourself are a misguided roman tic who struggles to intellectually justify his presence on earth.'

'But Patrick was a romantic too,' I protested, still coughing.

'Patrick's romanticism was of a completely different kind: his romanticism was motivated by the desire to see himself before he became self-aware, as a pure phenomenon, as a wonder. Have you read his last play? Oh, no? What a pity! There he has the ... the ... the ... apotropiastic lines: *I am for magic. For dream. For love. That pervasive dream which becomes more real than reality if we have faith in it.* I call them *apotropiastic* because they repel evil thoughts, pessimism and death. A simple truth can destroy civilizations.'

He talked with passion, his eyes big and dark, shining with purity. Those eyes and 'the ... the ... the ... apotropiastic lines' by Patrick transformed our meeting.

Yes, I was still coughing.

When I arrived home three hours later, I tried to find the play. *Shepherd on the Rocks:* what a disarming exorcism!

The stench of life

It took several weeks for those chips to be digested. My throat still burnt. I went on an excursion with some visitors up to the Blue Mountains. When I returned home there was a brief message on my answering machine. I called back. He didn't ask about my disappearance. He simply began:

'I forgot to tell you last time we met about Alexandria and myself. I don't like to look exotic, but I must tell you that any interest in me must begin with my own incompleteness. Out of neglect, I deified an absent mother, and out of fear I worshipped a remote father – as if such feelings could account for my incompleteness. The only permanent conclusion I managed to extract from that life is about the unpredictability of things. Can you see a traumatic childhood here? I don't really remember it, and honestly have forgotten all about it. Deep in our inner self, you know, there is nothing else but us, now. But the dreadful, beloved mediocrity of our families can create monsters. Mediocrity has a single debilitating effect: it leaves no space for forgiveness.'

There was a brief pause as he pulled his thoughts together. Deep breath.

'I hope that the chips we had the other day were kind to you, because they gave me bowel problems for days. Next time you visit me we will go elsewhere.

That restaurant is expensive and not very good. Come and see me soon. I hope that you are not off to Greece again? How can you afford such frequent trips?'

His back was bad too, and he told me to call him again in a few days. I did so three weeks later.

'Have you been away again?' he asked.

'No, no,' I replied. 'Simply busy with work. So many paper wars for nothing. My heart is swollen; it's rather pathological.'

He didn't register that.

'The problem of our life today is that we understand all too well what needs to be done but we never take the appropriate decisions, no? Chekhov said in one of his letters that *nothing is clear in this world. Only fools and charlatans know and understand everything.* You must decide. Don't let life submerge you in its currents and make you unable to react.'

I thought this was slightly ironic, coming from him.

'Don't be fooled by romantic notions of freedom, revolt and (how do they call it these days?) self-invention? I was always a minimalist in life: the only real hope for society is to make better gardens. As Voltaire said in his *Candide: Cela est bien dit, mais il faut cultiver notre jardin.* Only then do we pay more attention to the real shaper of our life, the weather. Have I talked to you about the weather in Patrick's novels?"

'You have.'

'Well, *repetitio est mater studiorum,* as the Romans used to say. We live in what is called a "demotic society" which turns creative people into internal exiles, taking them away from their own centres. But even then we need a lot of irony. Because aristocrats can be so cruel. The vulgarity of the lower classes is no match for their cruelty. We have to find our way between these alternatives. What did we do? We chose each other.'

'But don't you think that such privatization leaves society orphaned from its best people?'

'Maybe. But some day the critical moment in your life arrives when you have to do the wrong thing. Not because you must live to regret it, but because under the circumstances the wrong thing can be very positive. From it you must extract the central moral virtue: forgiveness. Forgiveness is strength.'

I was puzzled. 'I don't know if something like that is possible, under the circumstances. Forgiveness indicates powerlessness, or romanticised Christianity. Most of the time I cannot even contemplate forgiveness.'

'Obviously you have not been exposed to evil; that's why you cannot forgive. Patrick and I experienced the devastating experience of War and we know that the only truth possible afterwards is that we may never know the place we will be buried. War shatters everything: your humanity, your identity, your body. You are not the same person after War; you are a ghost. Like the souls in Homer: they must drink blood in order to remember. We tried desperately to forget, out there at Castle Hill, and before that in Greece, but to no avail.'

He stopped and added, his voice firm and revelatory:

'I am telling you: forgiveness is redemption! Keep that in your mind. Those unable to forgive live in a demonic anxiety which makes them lose self-control. They *become* evil, gradually and unconsciously, because the inability to forgive gathers in you everything negative, nullifying, misanthropic.'

I thought I heard sighs. Why? There must have been something personal in all this that evaded my understanding.

'Can I visit you this weekend?' I asked.

'Definitely, but call first to confirm. Those dreadful chips inflamed my bowels and it is not a pleasant experience being close to me these days.'

'Don't worry, Mr, Lascaris,' I said. '*The stench of life makes everything real.*'

'That's not yours,' he laughed. 'That's most obviously Patrick's, no?'

'Most obviously.' I had crossed the line again. His love of superlatives depressed me so much that I adopted it wholeheartedly, despite the fact that he had accused me of overdoing them.

'Most abominable, most impressive, most unacceptable' with the intonation of a voice in love with polysyllabic words.

It was most edifying indeed.

The crossing

'It depends on what you do with what you have, or with what you are – every moment of your life. Accidentals define the essence.'

He used the Aristotelian term *sumbebhkovta,* which puzzled me. I didn't know that he read philosophy, or indeed Aristotle. I suppose it was for the allure of the ancient language.

'What is our essence, Mr Lascaris?' I dared ask. 'Some time ago, you told me that we don't *have* an essence.'

'You must have very few things to do in your life if you remember that. Essence means fulfilment or realization. It follows rather than precedes you. Whatever is external that makes you become yourself is your essence; it does not come from within you; it does not belong to you. It comes from outside to the extent and degree that it finds a way of entering and growing roots in you.'

Oh, his deep breath!

'For example, everything that causes emotions: fear, attraction and so on, strikes a chord in us which generates feelings we alone can experience. We are all afraid in different ways. These things have nothing to do with you. You gather yourself around centres of convergence not otherwise possible, nor even able to be imagined.'

'What sort of centres?' I asked, curious. This sounded mystical but I couldn't say the word.

'Well, emotions are our defences against reality or even the primordial inhabitants of the mind. The centres of our life are outside our self. After we open our eyes, the first thing we do is fight against the attraction of a pestilential mother, or the gravity of a miasmatic father. Very few people realize that our primal cry is an attempt to avoid the black emptiness of our presence in the feelings of our parents.'

'I wouldn't know, Mr Lascaris,' I said. 'I grew up with my grandmother, who was all peace and grace.'

'That explains your unsophisticated way of thinking. The cardinal sin in our century is a happy childhood. Those who had one have destroyed the world.'

He gazed deeply into my eyes.

'How does it feel to have had a happy childhood?' he asked.

'Well, it makes you unaware of fear and panic,' I said. 'It gives you a thread that connects you to the incoherence of life to come.'

I wanted to continue with stories about my grandparents, but he shook his head in despair.

'Mr Vrasidas, I understand now why you cannot become an adult. And maybe why you will dare any heroic deed. You remain suspended in a perpetual crisis of faith and identity, devoured by the scepticism born out of the lack of tragedy in your own life.'

This was really tough. Yet, deep down, I felt it was a true and authentic picture of my mind. I tried to hold my ground.

'With due respect, Mr Lascaris, I suspect that you want everyone to feel some sort of masochism through suffering and guilt, in order to be themselves. Aren't you projecting on to others the misadventures of your own life? Is this fair?'

He stopped and laughed with cruel sympathy.

'My dear ignoramus, we are not pursuing suffering. It is out there – and if you are lucky enough to meet it, you gain self-consciousness. It imposes limits and responsibilities. In the Catholic Church it is called 'grace', despite the fact that they see it as a beatific vision. In reality, it is in your most humiliating moment that grace is bestowed upon you. Only then do you lose everything: your defences, excuses and alibis, and regain the nakedness of your birth. Then you gain self-consciousness: you become known to your mind.'

I sighed with relief. What he said was beautiful, cruel, horrific. It made me lose the best part of my innocence, and that was good and just and liberating.

'Mr Lascaris,' I said, 'I am really grateful to you for sharing your thoughts with me.'

'What?' he exclaimed in horror. 'Are you out of your mind? I am simply healing wounds which you cannot see or even feel. It is sad, my dear friend. There is no reason to be grateful unless you suffer from that ... that sort of *maaaasochism* you mentioned before. It is really sad.'

He paused. That deep breath again.

'By the way,' he frowned, 'what is the Greek word for *maaaasochism?*'

'*Masochismoooos,* if I am not wrong.'

'It seems that things are worse than I suspected. Is it possible that the language of Plato does not possess a word for that notion, and has to borrow the name of an obnoxious marquis in order to express it? How is that possible?'

'Well it is, Mr Lascaris,' I replied. 'Greeks borrowed the notion because they don't have the experience. They are not *maaaasochists,* they are only *saaaadists—*'

He gazed at me with repugnance.

'I cannot sustain a serious discussion with you,' he said, shaking his head.

We were strolling through Centennial Park. It was early evening, on an Arctic September day. Suddenly the wind started blowing with great force: dust and leaves in the air, dark clouds appearing from nowhere. The first drops of a Sydney storm sprinkled our skin.

'Let's run back home through the crossing,' he said. 'It's faster.'

Around the Park is an old iron fence protecting the green haven from intruding cars. In order to get into the Park, you have to go around it. That takes ten minutes. But thirty metres further on from where we stood, two iron rails are missing, and through this gap, Lascaris, his dog and his friends would squeeze each time they went for a walk.

The storm made us run as fast as we could. When we arrived at the gap, Milly jumped first and crossed over the Martin Road footpath. The rain started pouring down. Mr Lascaris usually let me go first, following with a sardonic paternal smile. But on that occasion, without thinking, we both hurled ourselves simultaneously through the gap. We stuck, joined back to back, both trying to push through. He stopped out of astonishment; I stopped out of confusion. Neither knew who would make the first move.

Milly started barking at me. She ran up and bit my hand. I heard nasty words coming out of my mouth. The rain soaked us, relentlessly. Two stray dogs appeared on the other side of the fence, inside the Park. They started growling, showing us their teeth.

Milly turned from my hand and attacked them ferociously from the protected side of the fence.

We stood for over a minute, each expecting the other to move first. Some kids, rushing for cover on their bikes, shouted at us: 'Weirdos go home!'

'Mr Lascaris,' I said patiently. 'Please move first. We're making a spectacle of ourselves.'

I kept still as he pushed his right shoulder backward, causing me considerable pain. As he dragged his left foot out with his usual slow majesty, I bounced forward, breathing free at last. My chest was aching and my hand was bleeding from Milly's sharp teeth.

'This is a charming incident,' he said, straightening his clothes. The rain still saturated us. The thick lenses of his antediluvian glasses were streaming with water.

Suddenly he stopped. Solemnly and calmly he turned to me, raising his right hand in its commanding position.

'From this moment we shall call this opening the Lascaris Crossing. It indicates the impossible symbiosis between dissimilar people.'

I could sense the immense euphoria of his whole body. Mine had already started shivering.

He is christening the place, I said to myself. Oh, gods what else?

'Yes, the Lascaris Crossing, whatever–' I consented impatiently. 'Can we go now? I'm prone to pneumonia, and I don't want this crossing to be the final one of my life–'

He laughed. We went back to the house. The rain stopped at the very moment we entered it. He gave me some ancient towels to dry myself. I left soon after.

I stayed in bed for almost a month, suffering from bronchitis. He called me once or twice, but I didn't reply.

When we made contact again, he said with his usual irony:

'More adventures of the most trivial nature?'

Was I looking for a father? Had I been so deprived of fear and anxiety that I needed to project on to him the attention and approval I needed in order to relive my childhood and establish relations of some value?

As Patrick White would have said: 'Oh, nooooo–'

Stay calm. Don't panic!

War

I was not looking forward to our next meeting. When I arrived, it was a sunny imperial day. We went for a walk around his neighbourhood so that he could show me the mansions of certain wealthy Greeks. But I was there for different reasons. War and power had been persistently in my mind, as I tried to interpret Voss' impenetrable personality.

My mood was sober and my face sullen. I was very disappointed that Keating had been defeated in the elections.

Mr Lascaris was in confessional mood. He started with a dream from earlier that week.

'Optimists are those who do not trust experience,' he pontificated.

I thought that this oracular tone would determine our meeting. I was slipping deeper into the abyss of melancholia. He continued:

'I had a dream that I was a child in my aunt's house in Academias Street in Athens. A guest came in, someone I shouldn't have seen: whispers and hushed voices. My nanny took me out for a walk to the Royal Gardens. I walked in front. When I turned, my nanny had disappeared, as if absorbed by the greenness of the trees. I ran back home in tears. The huge house was empty. I struggled to climb the stairs to my room. They seemed to expand before me. I also felt that someone was staring at me. "Who are you?" I asked in panic. My distorted voice echoed through the house. Then my Aunt Despo in her fashionable designer clothes stood on a cushion of clouds and was taken up to heaven through the ceiling. I was left totally alone in the room. I looked around and saw trophies hanging on the wall. They were the different limbs of my body. I had been dismembered, and yet was fully conscience of my self.'

'Mr Lascaris,' I said, 'you are very Freudian in this dream!'

He ignored this comment.

'As time passes, I realize how misleading dreams are. And we are attracted to anything that misleads us, no? Life is sustained by the way we whisper small and petty secrets – the way we whisper, I repeat. My childhood was the prelude to greater catastrophes: Asia Minor, expulsion, exile, migration. Everywhere a foreigner. Even with my own kind, it seems to me that we are all born among hypothetical beings, constantly testing their reality through our fears and insecurities. As we grow older, we tend to surrender to the gravity of illusions. When a real human being emerges, we realize how lost we have been and how seduced we have been by ghosts and phantoms. Such realization is our first step to becoming moral.'

The deep breath again.

'Affection – yes, affection, as Patrick said' – heavy breathing. 'It is all that remains.'

And what about me, his listener? But yes, I was deeply seduced by the path he followed to discover his truth.

'What about your adolescence in Athens?' I asked.

'Athens! A dreadful city! I still remember being called "the foreign seed" and, as you understand, even now I refine the vulgar expression of our fellow Greeks. What a coarse nation we are! What a tribe of uncivilized savages!'

'I know what you mean,' I replied. 'That's the reason I left that country with no intention of returning.'

'The problem with all catastrophes is that they are never, unfortunately, final. We survived and moved to Egypt, nurturing the dream of lost homelands. And then came the War. As I must have told you, we are the children of War. Pain, loss, absence, familiar buildings burnt down, names of friends and lovers on the list of those missing in action. No perspective. No future. No hope. Caught in each minute as in a lethal trap. Death comes as liberation. Thrown into a century of panic. Desire, loss, merged into the khaki uniform of the Army. Distant machine guns. Bombardment. The rattling and humming of chthonian deities ready to cannibalize your most precious moments. War is the ultimate distorter of our mind.'

'Wow, Mr Lascaris,' I exclaimed, 'that's real stream of consciousness!'

He ignored this.

'And then among all that: Patrick. The only real being forcing me to make choices and become myself. His art made my catastrophes useful, because we lived every moment as a long good-bye, which each one had to say in order to see the light of the next day. Was it back in 1941 or 1942 when we met? Everything is so blurred.'

He started again.

'Well, contrary to that existentialist rubbish, art records our submission to destiny. Was everything in vain? You have to see the way we lived under the shadow of War. His books were compasses for our journey through nothingness. Our generation was emotionally mutilated. Art is not the fine thoughts of refined minds. It records the missing parts of our body, of our mind. Art is the necessary catalyst for purity and completeness.'

I wanted to protest about existentialism. I moved my hands in front of his eyes. He kept ignoring me.

'*Buuuut* despite all that, we had to imagine our destiny after the War. Having lost all illusions, what became the most solid, the most permanent presence before us? Our frail and mortal, sinful body. Affection, yes. That's what I loved in Patrick. Those who haven't lived through the ravages of War are unable to understand what it means to live an uneventful life in the suburbs or the provinces. *Buuuut,* I am telling you: it means bliss and transfiguration, fighting ghosts and creating myths and confronting memories, through mopping, cooking, washing, dining in silence.'

He sighed with relief, looking intensely into my eyes.

'I'm sorry that I present myself through such romantic contrasts. Patrick noticed a certain "fatality", as he called it, in me – but please do not take it as fatalism. Very few words remain credible any more, and yet we have to make complete sentences with them.'

No, no,' I said, 'keep talking! Your romanticism is very neo-classical indeed.'

'You are very witty for a Greek,' he added. 'Where did you learn the art of being epigrammatic?'

'Studying at the University of Athens,' I said. 'A ghastly place – but I did have to learn many classical authors by heart, so it helped me build a good memory.'

This meant nothing to him. Deep breath. He concluded:

'Some people think that we remained so private because of our carnal engagement. I must tell you that we remained so distant because of the War. We had been infected by that dreadful virus of fear, inhumanity, cruelty. We were the products of a collective crime, of a devastating black death that deformed the calmness of our natures and the willingness of our hearts to communicate. Yes, I know. We were not like the Jews who suffered so much and have therefore become the moral arbiters of human conscience. I recognize the higher moral authority of the most insignificant Rabbi anywhere on this planet, so much higher than the arrogant Pope in Rome or our miserable Patriarch in Constantinople. During that War, every human being was transformed into a demon, into a cannibal. As the ancients said, nature was transformed for us from divine to demonic. Our chosen solitude was the only way to purify our existence from the stains of experience.'

'Mr Lascaris,' I dared, 'you sound so pessimistic.'

'Yes, indeed – and I don't want to change. I'm pessimistic because I know that irrespective of how many times you sweep the floor, dust and grit always prevail. Isn't that enough? Are you using a vacuum cleaner?'

He was making fun of me. It was time to go.

'I still think that John Howard as Prime Minister is not a very good thing at all,' I said.

He looked at me with sympathy.

'We survived Hitler,' he said abruptly. 'In the end, Howard looks pretty insignificant.'

With grave solemnity, he continued:

'You must remember, impetuous young man, that all our words are about corpses, corpses of friends, of people we desired, of things we lost. We do not feel sadness: we see sadness. All our feelings are objects in front of our eyes.'

'But each generation has its own dilemmas to confront and resolve,' I said in a subdued voice.

He looked at me with pity and contempt.

'Everything flows in liberating randomness. Our life is flooded with tides beyond our control. We surrender, and for many years we collect ropes and nails to fasten our existence to oceans without visible islands, and distant lights. Have you ever felt like that?'

I was about to say something about growing up in an unstable society in the 1960s, but realized this was crass and somehow irreverent.

'From our meetings and long discussions I urge you to remember only this sentence,' he told me, his hand raised in its commanding position indicating that I had to shut up.

'I repeat: what can be said must be silenced. You must remain quiet about the things that concern you the most, and talk through your silence. Do you understand?'

Well I didn't – plus it reminded me of Wittgenstein's sentence. I had failed his philosophy four times in exams. A feeling of visceral confusion was gradually emerging in me.

'Mr Lascaris,' I said, my voice trembling, 'each generation faces different problems and deals with them differently.'

This was really stupid and obnoxious, but I felt I had to say something.

He responded violently.

'We had to face problems created by others. Can't you see the difference?'

I could see it and knew what he meant. But I couldn't explain the violence in his voice. That tone depressed me so much, that after I left I had double fish and chips. Soon the effects began and I started vomiting, alone somewhere in Centennial Park.

I heard scuffling noises: people having sex in the bushes. I passed out. In my dream, I saw Michael Dransfield's giant dog flying over Sydney, and then the poet himself whispered in my ear: *another silence. a voice in a bright labyrinth, a prison of colour.* It was Lascaris' voice. I stayed unconscious in cosmic gratitude for the whole night. Without realizing it I was making myself into one of Patrick's unclubbable characters.

He disoriented me. I felt grateful.

Of countries old and new

It took a long time to recover. But after that discussion, I decided to take any opportunity to ask him about Australia.

'Listen, young man,' he said impatiently, 'to me, Australia means one thing alone: salvation. Don't ever believe those stupid ideas about roots, uprootedness and displacement. Absolute rubbish! Some people are paid for such nonsense. Australia saved me from ghosts and demons, liberated me from paternal protocols of obedience, gave a new rhythm to my quest for meaning. Please spare me talk about "the old country!"'

'What do you feel about it?'

'We Greeks are one of the most unfortunate calamities to have befallen humanity,' he exclaimed, in such archaic Greek that he reminded me of Plato's melancholy in his Seventh Epistle.

'We are despicable,' he said, using the magnificent Greek word *a-ka-ta-no-ma-stoi,* which in English means un-nameable.

'Despicable because unjust!' he forged on. 'No one has ever taken responsibility for the disasters we have inflicted upon ourselves. No one! We lost our capital: we lost Smyrna, we lost everything – and no one has ever taken responsibility. We are an anti-political nation. And do you know what? We are anti-political – us, the inventors of politics – because we don't have a sense of tragedy! I have told you before (was it you?) that we invented tragedy in order to play operetta! That's what we're doing. And some people think that this is good and shows our exceptional character. The only thing it shows is that we are artificial and bucolic – another Greek word with ambiguous connotations!'

'That's a bit ungenerous, Mr Lascaris,' I protested.

'Don't you think we have shown enough kindness so far? You are from the old Greece and have never felt what it means to leave behind the port of Smyrna, silently saying a long and irrevocable good-bye. My family did exactly that. I live with these memories to this day. And who was responsible for this? Greek politicians! And what happened to them? They thrived and prospered and still rule the country. We are a nation unable to face the truth; isn't this enough to condemn us for ever? We have not been pierced by the sharp nails of conscience. Our forehead is wrinkled only by the sun. Thinking is not a part of our existence. We live in the mythological space of fairy tales. That's why I'm telling you: irrespective of how many of Patrick's books you will translate, there is no basis in Greek for receiving his trembling awareness of tragic sublimation. Can you understand that?'

I became defensive. I retorted:

'Maybe – but what about Australia? Isn't it the same here?'

'Well, with due respect,' he replied, regaining his usual reserve, 'no. As a matter of fact, not at all. Australia is a country in which freedom exists because of human confrontation with the dilemmas of survival. But beyond that – which must be really deep for you – I must tell you: Australia gave me more than I asked for, more than I expected, more than I hoped for. Through that excess of offering I have myself become more generous, more open, more accepting. Generosity of emotion is, I believe, the only divine quality to which humans can aspire. Anything else follows.'

I was puzzled and a bit annoyed; I was thinking of my mother. He looked at me with a smile.

'You look puzzled and a bit annoyed,' he said stressing 'a bit', and using a diminutive word from the vernacular. 'I know – sometimes the vernacular provides the most immediate form of communication! But please can you forget your mummy for a while? She has her own loneliness to deal with!'

'Mr Lascaris,' I responded stiffly. 'Can you read my mind?'

'But you are so easy to read, young man. So easy!'

I had had enough. I got up. He noticed that I was about to cry.

'In our comfortable mediocrity, these tears are nothing compared with what my family felt when they were leaving the harbour of Smyrna. My family and so many other families.'

'I know that, Mr Lascaris,' I said, somehow aggressively. 'My whole life has been a long good-bye to the only mother that keeps me linked to my childhood: our Greek language. And I know that I will also have to farewell her one day. I have no other way of renewing myself.'

I was tense and abrupt.

'It will be tragic,' he said softly, touching my head gently with his left hand. 'But it may also be necessary if you want to discover your place in the scheme of things.'

He understands me, I thought. He knows what I'm talking about.

'Yes, I understand you very well,' he continued as I was left wondering. 'You know, of course, that we are fascinated by what we deny. This fascination makes everything nobler. When your voice breaks, when your mind hesitates, when you feel trapped, then you are struggling with yourself, to redeem your nature from your conditioning. It is noble, purifying, beautiful.'

His voice was a flat, monotonous, Byzantine chanting. I was transported and felt suddenly at home in our common exile. This was the first time I kissed his hand when we said good-bye, in the same way I used to do with the priest in our little town, when I was innocent and frightened.

'That was so religious, young man,' he called from the top of the footpath. 'So religious! You are on the wrong path!'

I had always guarded my faithlessness religiously. But he could see through all that and appreciate the importance of the religious.

The spirit

It was probably the last time I saw him alone. The day offered a Sydney epiphany. It was translucent, suggestive. He offered me tea.

'You must learn to drink tea,' he admonished. 'Coffee makes people nervous.'

Very cruel vicious advice to a coffee addict.

'We were talking the other day about the War,' he continued. 'Probably I gave you the idea that I am resentful and bitter. *Buuuut,* remember: we Greeks have no politics because we have underestimated the spirit. Political life presupposes spiritual quest – and that's what we are missing.'

'Don't forget,' he added in a louder voice, 'that every human adventure, whether public or the most private, is about atonement, about redemption, about restoration.'

He said *apokatastasis,* that most Homeric word of the New Testament, stressing each syllable. The polysyllabic became suddenly alive.

He took a deep breath and continued:

'And yet we always long for what we lose. Sometimes the best part of us is indeed our sinfulness and moral ugliness. Yes, I know it is blasphemous – but on many occasions it is true.'

136

'What do you mean?' I asked in a state of confusion. 'Restoration means to retrieve our completeness without the fragmentation of sin. How can we long for our sinfulness if, as you say, all adventures are about redemption?'

He smiled sardonically.

'It is paradoxical, isn't it? But you presuppose the dichotomy between flesh and spirit. Let me ask you something: is the spirit as innocent, pure and good as many have claimed?'

'Well, no, but–'

He shook his head.

'And is the flesh so guilty of all sins? Let me tell you something: mental sins are the most serious, the most destructive, the most luciferian. Spiritual pride, egotism, cruelty, for example, are lethal. This is elementary in any catechism. How can I condemn a prostitute or a junkie when they have been unable to take control of their life since their childhood, or after they have lost control over themselves through their passions? I must tell you that today all those who speak of God are spiritually dead. God has become the most un-spiritual word today, full of destructive hatred and misanthropic contempt. For me, religion is the love of death, a death-wish for ourselves and others. I mean, of course, religion as a social institution, because lonely recluses, hermits and mystics redeem life from its excess of sin and transform our natural propensity for evil into a quest for elevating awe.'

'That reminds me,' I said, interrupting his reverie, 'of an essay by Patrick on belief. Are you one of the sources of his religiosity?'

'Mr Vrasidas, you are impossible!' he shouted derisively. 'How can you find sources for your life in the belief of others? Each one of us begets faith afresh, as personal withdrawal. You must withdraw from life in order to become a believer. And you know when that happens? When someone questions your own legitimate existence. Only then can you feel the edges of your body and understand your presence. Young man, enter the desert and then reality will bloom!'

'Impressive, Mr Lascaris, but very Christian,' I added impatiently, 'but look at the history of the church from its beginnings until today. It is either anti-spiritual despair or coercion that leads people into its bosom.'

'I know what you are trying to say so badly,' he told me. 'It is true that, historically, Christianity defeated all heresies in the fourth century. Then it was immediately taken captive, while victorious, by imperial power. Another religion! Very few people understand that power is a religion in itself, but cannot exist autonomously. It must take over something else, like a parasite. So power took over Christianity in the most tragic pseudomorphosis in history. So many centuries of deception – and still we pay the price!

Yet most of us baptized Christians are unaware of such betrayal. We struggle to be good and compassionate while the whole structure of our religion is an enormous chimera.' 'I know what you mean,' I said. 'Christianity should have remained in the catacombs, the religion of slaves. After it came out to become the religion of the imperium, it went downhill fast.'

'Oh God – you are really funny with your over-simplifications!' he replied. '*Buuuut* we cannot retain our illusions about any organization, you know. If we lose what is in front of our eyes, it is better to return to animism. We must respect objects – all objects. Their existence gives us identity and therefore faith. Who was the Greek philosopher who said *everything is replete with gods?* He was so true and so honest.'

'So do you believe in God or gods?' I asked, intrigued by his paradoxical language.

'As I grow older I have less and less faith – which means I need to believe more and more. Because when you give an answer to a problem, the problem itself changes. After you give an answer to the question of God, for example, the "God-question" itself becomes something else. The fact that *you* are asking transports you into the question itself; it makes you part of it.'

'I don't really follow you,' I whispered.

'How can I express it,' he wondered, 'without your calling me a mystic, as before? Your questions themselves place you within the spiritual continuum which ultimately makes our fragmentation meaningful.'

He used the Greek word ρευστόν, which means fluid liquid, and is indeed a mystical term. He went on:

'Your mind will change radically when you see yourself as a guest. Only then each moment blooms in us as emotions and mindscapes. When we feel, nothingness – our daily nothingness – is transfigured into life. I was born at the end of the period reaching back to the 1890s when Wilde proclaimed that the aim of life is self-development. Well, I always thought of him as somebody who wasted his very many talents. Life is about meetings; it has nothing to do with you as an individual. Through meetings we become able to articulate the seemingly incomprehensible words through which our soul makes irrational, impossible claims on reality. We don't need religions: we need friendships, loves, passions. Yet at the moment your body feels alive, then you are "religious"!'

His Greek words were heavy, measured – and startling.

'Yes, it's through such meetings that we can say "love" for example, or "hope" or "truth" – and these are quite irrational. Can I be witty? Well, I shall be. Love ends when we fall in love. And hope is undesirable martyrdom. Truth is what we try to avoid. Is that enough? I must go on. I am talking about experience now, and not about ideas and concepts, right? Can I tell you something? We use these words because we are afraid of their opposites, not because we live them. I always wondered if we depict beautiful things and people simply because we want to avoid omnipotent ugliness. We don't like beauty in itself. Beauty is demoralizing, cruel, destructive. We say that we are after beauty, but in reality we are running away from ugliness – our ugliness. That's what Patrick's books tried to illustrate. His works avoided grappling with our greatest fears, because they are everywhere. In Patrick's works you can't find saints because sanctity is beyond representation. Therefore – and I will finish with this, young man – only through our ugliness can we understand the meaning of life. I have said it before – but never mind. I feel I have to repeat it.'

Oh dear me, I thought, he is preaching! But why?

'Would you like some more coffee now?' he asked politely. His voice became soft, velvety, numinous. Through his coffee he was trying to tell me something which was beyond my horizons.

'Mr Lascaris,' I said, 'as we say in Greek, your mind is extremely heightened today.'

'What an expression!' he sighed in admiration. 'When we feel premonitions, it's as if we come out of ourselves, no?'

'What sort of premonitions?'

'It's so many years after Patrick's death and the publication of his biography,' he said pensively, 'and it seems to me as if his work has almost been forgotten, as if it has been relegated to the level of literary references. With due respect to those present, academics have now destroyed any sense of literary sensitivity.'

'Oh, Mr Lascaris,' I protested. 'We just study literature from a different perspective.'

'We? We?' he repeated with an expression of shock on his face. 'Don't tell me that you have joined their ranks?'

'By definition, Mr Lascaris, I am one of them.'

'Well I hope that your mind has not been polluted and totally destroyed. I hope that you have maintained your good sense – thanks I hope to your "frequentations" here.'

What a word! 'Where did you excavate that word from?' I asked in amazement.

He smiled.

'You don't read Thucydides, young man,' he exclaimed. 'You would learn so much if you read him more often.'

'Can I bring a friend with me next time?' I asked.

'As long as he is not like the other one,' he said, exasperated. 'It was very sad to see you degrading yourself so much for something so cheap. You know what I mean when I say *something* –'

'This is very moralistic, Mr Lascaris,' I said.

'Honest nevertheless!' he exclaimed.

He looked around with some discomfort.

'Have I ever told you about my understanding of death?' he suddenly asked.

'Oh, no, no–'I mumbled.

'We must find an opportunity for that. I feel so exhausted after talking with you – as if I have been pushing a loaded cart uphill.'

It was time to go. For the first time I noticed his shoes and mismatched socks, one dark blue and the other plain black, frayed and rather smelly.

That's the smell I notice every time I come to the house! I realized.

Next time, I would ask Alkis to come along.

When Manoly met Alkis

Alkis had a quirky way of walking. Like a colourful Anna Pavlova, balanced on cat's paws, he glided along Glebe Point Road every day at noon. He was going to collect the mail for the government agency for which he worked.

He appeared at the office around eleven and left just after two. Then he was suddenly dismissed from the job without pay, a truly great achievement for a government employee.

He usually dressed in a canary yellow shirt, orange trousers and a green British jacket. His shoes were half black, half white in the best fashion tradition of the Al Capone generation. He appeared in my office, without an appointment, wanting a translation: Greek through and through. The translation was only a pretext.

A strange story about being infected with AIDS. Outside Thessalonica at three o'clock in the morning, June 1989, in the middle of nowhere. Pitch black darkness. A tall, muscular, blond god appeared from the abyss: a middle-aged pilot from Australia. Alkis had been returning from a ball dressed in traditional Tyrolean outfit, for milkmaids. On high heels and with his Swiss hat on, he had appeared as if he were looking for a cow to milk. No time for precautions.

In September that year, he arrived in Sydney. He and the pilot spent three months of ecstatic bliss. In December they went to Noosa on holiday. The blond god collapsed. Hospital. Diagnosis: inoperable pneumonia. Dead in four days. Alkis alone in Noosa. English no good. Doctors said: 'You have been infected.' Suddenly four strangers arrived. The woman said that she was the wife of the god. Three adults, their children, accompanied her. She told Alkis that he had to go. From then on, it was 'a strictly family affair'. Alkis cried. English no good. Doctors repeated: 'You were infected six months ago. Your partner had the virus for years.' Alkis cried. He took the bus to Sydney. He checked into a cheap hotel close to Taylor Square and cried for days. In his delirium he sang: *'Put the blame on me, boy, put the blame on me–'*

'Immortal Gilda! Why was I dressed as a Tyrolean milkmaid? Why not as Gilda, the only Jerusalem I have ever worshipped? *We shall never surrender ... I have a dream ... The end of the horizon is red...'*

He lived for another ten years.

How would Manoly react to such a story?

I never had the chance to tell him this demonic fairy tale.

(lapsus memoriae)

'The truth about us will be *seen* after our death,' Mr Lascaris told me that memorable day before he met Alkis.

I didn't see him alone again. But every time I went back to Greece, a homeland lost forever but revisited with a stoic smile, Manoly's voice echoed around me:

'Death is the great revelation; nothing else matters except the knowledge we give to others through our death.'

It was too Socratic for me. I detested the wizard of Athens who filled the human mind with so much irony that it hasn't ever recovered, and cannot regain its simple affirmation of life. But like Socrates, Lascaris was a wise old man who revealed unexpected truths through whimsical jokes and clumsy gestures. Wisdom for him was a kind of evasion, a diversion so that no one would discover the dark caves of his existence. He never really told me anything about Patrick as a person. He was protective, as if they had never actually been together; he was secretive, as if a cloud of unknowing had fallen over his memory and concealed what mattered most to him. I thought of such *aphanisis* as a special form of liberation, the kind brought to our life when a great absence befalls us.

A transformation took place when Alkis entered our lives. Then Mr Lascaris told us things about his private life with Patrick that can never be entrusted to print. He told us about his family and Patrick, their friends and acquaintances, and the arcane modulations of their private life. Somehow Alkis managed to unlock the repository where his memories hid. They tumbled out, vividly.

Something of an infatuation, I would say, if that didn't sound so horribly moralistic.

'He is so Greek!' Mr Lascaris exclaimed. 'Is he from Macedonia? They are so nationalistic up there!'

'Well, they have some problems with their neighbors,' I said, 'so they try to compensate.'

'He is so egocentric, too. We talked for two hours and he told me everything about himself – but never asked anything about me. He even told me that he doesn't care about Patrick's work! Such an elemental being! Without conflicts, without dichotomies! It is a Macedonian thing, isn't it?'

'As so many other things,' I said, pensively.

Alkis entered our lives like a whirlwind: demanding, relentless, insatiable. He was in a hurry. He knew that he was going to die soon. To be precise, he died seven hundred and twelve days after he met Mr Lascaris. He died as he turned forty, at the Royal Prince Alfred Hospital, surrounded by his friends and some noisy family members who had arrived in Australia to harvest the imaginary fortune he had made Down Under.

I never told Mr Lascaris that Alkis had died. I told him that he had decided to go back home – and that was true, since he had no other option but being sent back in a sealed coffin. He was buried in his native village away from the places where he met real love, and after he had found damnation.

Loneliness has its own logic and creates its own connections. I felt thrust aside by the closeness of the friendship that developed between them. Thinking that there must be something really deep in their relationship I had no option but to become an observer, their unofficial Eckermann.

In my recollections Manoly and Alkis gradually merge. Every time the three of us met for a Pan-Hellenic symposium, as we used to say, I was astonished by how like one another they were, the aristocrat from Byzantium and the peasant from Macedonia.

At the edge of their space I recorded their conversations, the discussion of two people now long dead, united in my mind by the melancholy of our last meeting in Centennial Park. We ate fish and chips and salad, and drank white wine in that cantankerous restaurant. On the way home, the two of them started talking louder and louder in Greek. They had a common enemy, their childhood.

Alkis said: 'Manoly, have I ever talked to you about my father?'

It was an electrifying moment. Silence followed. We stopped almost at the centre of the Park, where there are benches beside a small pool. The dazzling humidity

148

of Sydney lay all around us. Its gigantic flies crawled over our faces. The majestic dust of a prolonged drought sat grittily on our skins.

'Fathers!' I thought. 'This is a most interesting subject. I must concentrate.' Suddenly Alkis said:

'He raped me when I was twelve, and then passed me to my brother then to all the men in our village, for money. My mother knew what was happening but left me alone to deal with their rage and stupidity. While all these things were happening to me, my thoughts were flying to distant lands and blue seas and remote islands, where I could dance and sing without fear. All this lasted for less than six years. When I turned eighteen I escaped to Thessalonica. Big anonymous city: my salvation. There I could pray to the ephemeral deities of my life for forgiveness of those who had sinned against me. Being shallow protected me from internalizing all this morbid stuff; it saved me from my own history.'

Mr Lascaris and I listened to his confession with awe and fear.

'How do you remember your father now?' asked Mr Lascaris.

'He was an impotent cannibal!' he replied. 'He was punishing me for his own feelings of inferiority. And he was mean. I could clearly see that in his violence he was flagellating himself. I could feel his profound self-hatred in the way he abused me. It was his loathing of his own genitals that blinded his mind to what was making me suffer and scream.'

'Brave words,' Mr Lascaris said. 'It is so hard for us to accept that our fathers were once children – nasty children who never grew up. They may have suffered the same humiliations we went through, probably without our gift of self-consciousness. The blackness of their con science has always fascinated me.'

He remained silent after this. Alkis' hands shook. My happy childhood excluded me from the tragic beauty of their post-linguistic bonding.

Alkis continued:

'In Thessalonica, I discovered the lost games of childhood in the nocturnal pursuit of lust. I went with sailors, truck-drivers, hustlers. Years and years of complete self-oblivion, kneeling in front of faceless, wet, warm, wily godheads. I was playing with them. It was my childhood, misplaced and overturned, but still full of euphoric amnesia and intoxicating mindlessness.'

'Poor thing,' sighed Mr Lascaris. 'Thessalonica is full of churches which means that sin abounds. Sin is the only way that we can develop self-awareness.'

'Yes, self-awareness is an unhealed trauma,' said Alkis. 'People who know themselves are doomed to become saints. Their holiness is their personal death.'

'So true,' Mr Lascaris said. 'The first injustice ever com mitted simply made innocence impossible. I don't think that innocence exists. Our damnation is to kill innocence with our first experience.'

Alkis said: 'You are right. We can never experience innocence after we become aware of our body. And in order to defend our body against its history, we mythologize religions, ideologies and the rest. We search constantly for the fragrance of a substance which was destroyed immediately after we said "I am."'

Mr Lascaris said: 'As an old man, I am more interested in the skeleton and less in the flesh of things. You know that I saw my mother only twice in fifty years? She thought of my birth as a horrible anathema against her own life and faith. I tried to imagine her as a child: the Catechism in her hands, receiving her confirmation, her first Communion, her privileged upbringing in the States. Then my father enters: animalistic, profane, lustful. The sensual secrets of the bedroom became her only ways to feel her body. We have a body, you know! And it is sanctified and can be transformed and redeemed. We simply don't know it. *She* didn't know it. And she lost it. She lived for over sixty years, until her death, punishing her body for having produced me. Strange and paradoxical indeed. I never thought that my existence could have such an impact on somebody else's life. Thus *exeunt omnes,* as the Bard would have said, in a hurry and utter disgust.'

He touched Alkis' hand, complicit. He said:

'Our psyche remains an empty stage covered with dust, and echoing. No script or record of the performance exists and the actors have moved on to another theatre.'

He stopped, his eyes bewildered behind his dense glasses. He continued:

'You make me talk about so many unpleasant details of the indecipherable patterns of our lives. This is really good! So unlike our friend here' – indicating me–'who always forces me to rationalize everything.'

They laughed. I laughed.

We stood talking in the Park for hours, until the sun set and darkness fell over the trees. They were still talking about fathers, mothers and purification ceremonies, purposeless hedonism and devoted attachments. How could they even remember so many incidents?

They were nostalgic, I realized, even for their most painful memories. Tears fell to the ground as they invoked meaningless affairs and pointless episodes, indecent and crass and banal.

'Oh, no,' I thought. 'This is so Proust!'

Mr Lascaris said to Alkis:

'Our friend here thinks that we have risen from the pages of Proust.'

152

'Who is Proust?' Alkis asked.

'A French writer who loved fragrances and sounds, and everything moving.'

'Not for us, then,' Alkis said. 'I always dream of a Platonic kingdom of eternal immobility as my real home.'

'Our friend is bound to misunderstand us,' Mr Lascaris replied.

I felt so excluded from the conclave of their private tragedies.

Years after that meeting, when they are not here and I am elsewhere, I recall the verses of a minor writer:

Yet meet we shall, and part, and meet again,

Where dead men meet, on lips of living men.

Samuel Butler: a Delphic writer, appropriate for the occasion.

Silence

Sounds of unknowable entities: humans, animals, machines.

In the Park, inhaling the sunset, suddenly realizing, with blinding clarity, that we were living in a new land, unclouded by history. The sky's transparency, a thread back to existing.

Consumed, curious about each other though complete in ourselves. Invading each other's aura, gently.

Mr Lascaris paternally in front; Alkis next to me. Our steps scraping the slimy grass and swampy soil. The universe, inseparable from us. Having a self, yet sharing it, born out of sounds and unknown entities. The sun rolling away, we, there, sensing the vibrations of heat and fluidity that make life imaginable. The breath of an ineffable deity hovering over the leaves. The gaze of a departing myth hypnotising the insects that glowed in the air. The unforgettable weight of that moment.

Then urging out of the thick silence:

'Alkis, say something!'

Alkis' face remaining dark, sullen, ravenous, vulnerable, bony, already seeing another shore. Approaching the house. Lights on. The dog barking.

No word. The setting sun, stern, unimplicated.

Are you there?

'If we attempt a Kafkaesque reversal of perspective, how would the trees have seen us yesterday, Mr Lascaris?' I asked the following day.

The emotion of the previous meeting had been palpable. I needed to visit him again. Then Alkis arrived.

'We would have been something evil to those trees,' Mr Lascaris replied. 'Evil is the seduction of unintelligible things – and that's what we are to the rest of creation.'

Had he read Kafka too?

'You make me feel that we live in an animate universe which keeps an eye on our excesses,' I said.

'Very well put,' he applauded. 'But you must under stand something which has obviously evaded your thorough philosophical training and intense theological speculation. The basic truth of life stems from the reply you give to the most fundamental question of all questions. People like you lead everyone else astray.'

'Mr Lascaris, a truce please–' I implored.

'I continue: the history of all questions of the mind has been a misleading series of displaced formulations, such as *Does God exist?, What is the meaning of life?*

or even worse, *Who am I?* I might add some crucial moral questions – but I need a better questioner. There is only one question that needs to be answered, and it's the most naïve of all: *Are you there?* This is the primary question we have to wrestle with, both philosophically and existentially.'

I was taken aback. Through a strange series of synaptic connections, I remembered that this was the same question posed by pre-monotheistic religions. I told him so.

'Irrelevant!' he replied. 'The question is still unanswered. Certainly it is the emphasis that creates different philosophies and religions. Insist on the verb and you establish ontology. Insist on the pronoun and you have rationality. On the adverb, and pragmatism is born. I see the unity of all three in the question mark: it makes the whole sentence vibrate with redemptive confusion.'

He stopped.

'Do not forget,' he said, with his finger pointed into my nose, 'that even God asked Adam *Where are you?* after the first-born had tasted the fruit. Cute story, of course, but that's the essence of my question. *Are you there?* is the invitation to history.'

Alkis then spoke up.

'Manoly, the answer can only be an accident of life, a random, incongruous event that destroys the balance of our habits. It's the echo of your voice that will make the answer possible.'

I wanted to say something, but I knew too much about Thomas Aquinas to follow their *non sequiturs.*

Alkis added:

'Our virtues are probably the most horrible element in our character. They block the view of others and isolate us from the rawness of life. *Are you there?* to me means a dark road where I meet a beautiful stranger who offers me despair. I have the answer without ever imagining the question.'

I then started a completely different discussion:

'Mr Lascaris, I think that Patrick's novels answer this question you have just asked. I still remember the first paragraphs of *The Tree of Man:* the appearance of Stan Parker in the emptiness of the outback. So musical, pulsating, ruthless. I can never understand why there are people who don't like this book.'

'You are getting better! The answer is all over his work. It addresses not simply the fundamental condition of being alone, but also demonstrates an extraordinary ability to arrange language in a way that finds meaning. This question heightens our receptivity to the complexity of beings. You are transformed when you understand how important the sheer realization of this question is.'

Alkis started to say something else, totally unrelated to the situation. Forcefully, I retorted:

'Are *you* here, Mr Lascaris?'

An impregnable wall had been built which I didn't want to see. When the three of us were together, I preferred to go psychoanalytic instead of talking philosophy. In any case, Lascaris' question made me think about my inability to articulate my thoughts, and forced me to reconsider.

Are you there? A question addressed to all invisible presences.

Fathers again

'Yes, he left,' said Mr Lascaris, 'when I was young, and came back when I had grown up. Shadows falling over shadows. Grim and bleak silence. An absent beginning, growing up without reference points. Do we belong to our origins? Or is the purpose of life to detach yourself from them? If you want to be free and feel alive, then there is only one enemy: your beginning. That's what I think. The past is a sinister plot against our development.'

'Yet Manoly,' said Alkis, 'our beginning is the only certain thing we possess, and the only secure refuge to which we can return.'

'Yes, I know – but this is what I call escapism, infantilism. You have to break away; you have to recreate your reality, you have to revisit the experiences that made you exist as you are from another perspective. You have to see them through the eyes of another person, as I did, or through the life of anything that lies beyond your personal space. Happiness is found only in what you have already lost.'

They kept talking, absorbed and looking deeply into each other's eyes. I was somewhere in between, photographing their gestures, transcribing moments of silence, chronicling vibrations of invisible forces crystallized in deep breaths.

It was getting dark. I looked out: a tender, sentimental evening over Sydney. Years later I read Mishima's sentence: *To choose the place where one dies is the greatest joy in life.*

We understand the meaning of what happens in our lives long after those who live them are gone. That evening was like Socrates in Plato's *Apology:* desperate and sublime, regretful and compassionate.

I remembered Patrick's immortal line: *As the world darkens, the evil in me is dying.* My mind flooded with verbs.

Everything unsaid

Our final discussion left everything unsaid. We seemed to speak of everything but what we really wanted to say. Alkis was there, in a bleak mood. He moved around the house with an ease that I never dared imagine.

It was a winter evening, a landscape of farewell. When I left, I got into a cab whose driver told me he had slept with *that woman* in Greece.

'Do you know her? Mary her name. She was bloody hot,' he remembered in his singing Italo-Australian accent.

During the evening's discussion, Mr Lascaris had wanted to explore 'the unnerving shapes of incommunicable dreams'. He told me that God cannot be good or indicate harmony, order, unity. He insisted that 'God is the sum of our irresolvable dilemmas.'

He then attacked 'the cruel emptiness of human relations'.

'The Church Fathers define hell as the inability to look into each other's eyes,' he said. 'You, with your fancy words, would call it *incommunicability,* no?'

Then he moved on to 'the vulnerability of thinking in sincerity'. 'Thinking is self-castration when people forget history: you must agree with this!' he insisted.

He proceeded to the design of 'the sepulchres to the mothers that we have to build: they must be full of blank notebooks.' He talked about 'the insanity of early morning TV shows: you cannot enjoy the sun because of the confusion they cause!' Then he moved on to 'the enchanting objects of everyday life, like knives, cups and spoons'. He visited 'the phantasmal stillness of painful experiences'.

Finally he turned to me and asked about work, friends and prospects.

It was one of those times when I felt like an alien in this life.

His questions bombarded me.

'Have you decided to stay in Australia for good?'

'Do you have any friends here? Any emotional bonds?'

'Did you buy a house? Oh, no? But why not? You must have your own roof over your head!'

He was magnificent as he served me a cup of the usual fragrant instant coffee. Elegant movements: slow, introspective. His hands were shaking. I tried to taste, but something bitter curled my tongue.

He yawned; I understood I had to go. He said he felt tired, moody and lethargic. 'My medication, probably.'

It was only seven o'clock. Dark outside. Alkis finally sat down. He was thinner and thinner. Black circles around his eyes. Eczema on his hands and chest. The smell of bodily disintegration. Oh, that seductive smell of death!

I felt incense in the air; as if spirits were hovering over us; as if we were lying in hospital beds without nurses or doctors but on clean bright white sheets in a hollow reverberating room. We were sinking into the immaculate whiteness of linen.

Alkis said:

'I will stay a bit longer tonight, Manoly. I must tell you more about myself, because there is a small possibility that I will have to go back to Greece.'

Silence again. He looked straight into my eyes, almost begging me to leave.

I left the house silently and walked all the way to the main road where I hailed that cab. The driver was chatty:

'Paolo my name. Where you from, mate?'

'Greece.'

'I was there last year, on holidays. That's when I met that stunning woman, Mary, on the island of Hydra. Do you know it?'

'Yep, close to Athens.'

'That's it. That Mary was bloody'ot in bed! Ya know'er?' he yelled.

'The blonde girl from Hydra?' I guessed.

'Yep, yep – bloody'ot in bed–'

So the only remaining Greek on the planet was a desperate nymphomaniac. I was remembering Manoly's elegant, sorrowful, vulnerable movements.

What makes life possible

Manoly Lascaris never wrote anything, but he was a truly eloquent talker. He went directly to the heart of the matter, avoiding the periphrastic mannerisms of professional thinkers. He was a catalyst; his observations reduced everything to the basics.

No posturing. No novelty for the sake of it. Just shifts of position, perspective, relationship and thus of meaning. The unexpected emerged as the natural consequence of imponderable factors, which flickered for split seconds, then vanished. He was the master of the art of pointing out improbabilities. As an immigrant, he felt the uneasy compromise that one makes with a new society, a compromise based on half-truths and half-lies, evasions and revelations, desires and fears. He handled all that with the suspicion of the foreigner and the reserve of the aristocrat: not always a functional compromise. But it made him responsive to the slightest shades of emotion and grades of feeling. Everything for him seemed preverbal, existing in child-like innocence, an interesting contrast with Patrick White's writing. But language for him was the theatre of possibilities.

I glean from my notebook: *Humans meet because of their mutual dislike. What you learn unmakes you. Today we know the answers to all questions, so we must understand what the questions are about.* And more: *The eerie silence of the moment of reading shows that the writer has indeed entered your home.* Again: *Truth is anything that perpetuates existence.* And that penultimate statement: *Goodness is the decision you make in order to continue a relationship.*

'Any relationship, Mr Lascaris?' I asked.

'The relationship that rescues your heart from complacency and inclines you towards a good deed,' he answered.

As I read them now, they sound like witty aphorisms and moral truisms. But it was the intonation, the gestures, the eyes, that made every sentence a complete re-enactment of the situation, that gave birth to its meaning.

I didn't always understand what he was trying to tell me. He insisted that I must first fail tragically in order to understand his place in 'the scheme of things'.

'Contrition and compunction,' he said. 'That's what you need – but you can't have it. So you cannot really understand me. Yet I must tell you, that despite what you called my alleged pessimism, I have always been a very cheerful man, ready to crack a respectable joke.'

Talking on the phone, he said: 'If you want to understand Patrick's novels you must see them as extended parables which portray what I call "useful experience"– I mean useful to others.'

His hands pointed at me, didactically.

'Are you saying that the purpose of literature is utilitarian?' I dared.

'Any accomplished craftsman of words knows that whatever he says must have non-verbal consequences. These effects of language make life possible.'

First death

March 2001. Alkis had just died. I had vanished for months. I called Mr Lascaris; he was not well, he said. I felt guilty for having abandoned him for so long. How could I explain?

'Mr Lascaris,' I said, 'Alkis went back home, as he wished.'

'Home, home! Where is home for us?'

And then:

'Barbara is complaining about the royalties for the translation of *Voss.* She hasn't received anything from your Greek publisher.'

'And do you think I have been paid?' I retaliated.

Tension, unease. Silence again.

I wanted to tell him everything. Why I had disappeared for so long. Why I hadn't returned his calls. Why Alkis had left without a word. Yet it was that icy silence that deterred me, the implied feeling of rejection, anger for the privileges youth enjoys without deserving them.

Alkis had sworn me to silence. This oath had invented those invisible, alienating hieroglyphics of evasion. I couldn't say anything. I wasn't even to invite him to the hospital.

168

The previous weekend I had seen Alkis dying. Mardi Gras was spreading its noisy chaos over the city. He let out a guttural whisper, clutched the sheet, and was gone. He left behind his mortal vessel unfulfilled and yet emptied of everything. Bernard, the ultimate Samaritan, asked for a few minutes alone with his now uninhabited mortal skin.

The window was open and I could see the passionate city celebrating. Although there was so much noise around, I felt that I was dissolving in a heavy, pulpy, velvety dark substance, inhaling the departing essence of life through the vicious smells of the hospital, the sinister silence of the stars, the distressing hyperactivity of the doctor.

Abysmal silence; nauseating absence.

'Is this what death is?' I asked myself. 'Stiff waxen bodies smiling ironically?'

Mr Lascaris on the phone, waiting.

'Alkis had to go home,' I said again. 'His mother and brother were here and took him back, although I know he didn't want to go. He didn't have time to farewell you – but I'm sure that he meant to do it.'

My voice was shaking. Did he understand what I really meant?

'I must go to bed,' he said. 'It is late for me. I feel so tired. It's a pity that we didn't meet again, the three of us together, like that day in the Park. Then it was as if we were embodying time and inhabiting space, like a poem.'

I understood. Neither of us dared utter the dreadful word. His radio was on, and as if in a strange paroxysm of synchronicity, Sibelius' *Valse Triste* could be heard.

'Sibelius!' he called. 'Do you know that this short piece inspired Patrick during *The Eye of the Storm?* You have to read the novel as a verbal commentary on Sibelius' music.'

He was still there with me; he knew, but he didn't. Death had vaporized the magic and frivolity of our dialogues.

'Manoly, I will call soon,' I whispered.

'Good-bye!' he sighed.

It was three in the afternoon on Monday 12 March 2001. This was the last time we talked. It was the first time I had dared call him by his first name.

I had to escape. Death was all over me. My skin exuded the salty smell of tears and insomnia. That blackness every night, that cold in every handshake, that emptiness in every street. The paralyzing effects of nothingness. Loss of orientation, purpose, joy. Tasteless food, numbing water, formless dreams: the great gift of the senses anaesthetized.

Where else is home but in the body of someone you love? And only when death comes, do you understand displacement and absence. They leap into you, twisting your heart every time a familiar smell pierces the air. They become your only life. Their meaning transforms you.

But before that happens, you must make your own living choices: neither guided by tribal superstitions, rituals and idols, nor determined by reptilian attachment to land and possessions. Home is love for the corporeal, the palpable, the human, the humanizing, the impermanent. Yes, no, yes, *agape:* sharing, offering, yielding, partaking. *Agape, enantiodromia,* yes and no at the same time. You take it with you: *we loved each other and we hated each other.* Home is time shared in reciprocity. That's what Manoly Lascaris was trying to tell when he was writing on airy parchments or knocking back invisible enemies.

On the way, he had transformed me into a vapid moralizer. It was unfortunate. Why did I have to go through so much in order to confirm the trivial, elementary, stupid first article of every Christian Catechism? Sheer bad luck, I'm telling you, indifferent reader!

Australia suddenly became empty, a huge, timeless, barren land echoing with human desolation. I left for Greece and Holland, familiar havens. When months later I returned, I didn't try to see him again. When I used the phone, a female with a foreign accent told me that she would call me back. It must have been the nurse.

'Manoly, Alkis had to go home. He will have to stay there forever,' treading softy on the all-receiving earth.

But his voice came violent, impatient, manic:

'How impertinent of you to call me by my first name!'

He kept chastising me, even in my most private hallucinations.

His death

Manoly Lascaris died on 13 November 2003. I read the news in an Internet café in Athens. I don't know why, but Goethe's verse came immediately to my mind: *Die and dare rebirth!* As with all of us, death is an issue for those left behind.

I threw myself into Patrick's novels, struggling to discover the rhythms of Manoly's voice, the long intonation of his Greek vowels, his soothing voice under their centreless dialogues, his invisible dilemmas beneath their labyrinthine plots, his serene and stable gaze concealed by their chaotic complexity.

From David Marr's reconstruction of Patrick's life, I remembered the final remarks about 'a scruffy stretch of water' in Centennial Park which received the writer's ashes. I walked several times by that water, with Manoly's invisible presence.

Months later I discovered a battered notebook among my papers, stained with coffee. In it I had recorded my thoughts on Mr Lascaris and, in an act of enlightened self-transcendence, notes of what he had actually told me.

In retrospect, I felt guilty and petty. The great opportunity to see his life had been sacrificed on the altar of Promethean stupidity to learn about Patrick White's work. I could have done that by studying his books rather than talking to his partner, who had a life of his own! But it was too late.

But then something happened, and everything changed. Robert's mother had a stroke and was taken to Gosford Hospital. As we hovered beside her, in total weightlessness, with teary eyes and automatic movements, I could vividly hear Manoly's voice, impatient, supplicating, demanding. It sounds strange, and ectoplasmic – but I cannot refute my own senses. I was half-asleep, half-conscious, and the divide between the real and the over-there had collapsed. Manoly spoke clearly; I heard his smooth and tuneful voice, pleading like Hamlet's father: *Remember me ... Remember me.* And then, back in real time, it was nurses and doctors and trolleys all around, and nothing but that snaky pale susurration of absence. But I *heard* his voice. This was the closest I've ever been to his death and dying. The ineffable blackness seemed to take on a face, sorrowful and beseeching.

On the train backwards and forwards to the hospital from Central, I started reconstructing our shared moments. In the face of death, I could clearly sense the vibrating magnetism of his life.

So Manoly surreptitiously took possession of me. For months I struggled to understand. Gradually his words became material presences even though his bodily frame was not there to support them. His ghost started haunting me, every day. His voice emerged insistently from everything I read; slowly, gradually his presence became companion to all my explorations, in this world and the other. I found myself laughing whenever I remembered his characteristic expression: *Buuuut–* I copied it, mimicked it, mocked it. I felt satisfied that at last I was enjoying my revenge.

In several articles in Greek, I tried to recapture the spirit of his mesmeric personality, the vibrations of his voice, the tenacity of his gaze. I relived the funny way he used to hum the Greek national anthem, that sonorous piece of garbage that irreparably damaged my good taste. I recollected what he had told me about the notorious Greeks he had met in Australia in the 60s. I remembered his comments on Greek politics, his remarks about his family and his friends, about Australia, Patrick, their friends – and of course his sweet mockery of my existence.

'Please,' he implored me once. 'Don't record anything I'm telling you. I don't want people to feel hurt. I have lived my whole life noiselessly and I want to depart the same way.'

He used the beautiful Greek word $\alpha\theta\boxed{\times}\rho\upsilon\beta\alpha$, a truly aristocratic word, useful for all occasions when the mind is heightened. *Die and dare rebirth!*took on its full meaning.

Amid such confusion, I remembered the only thing he had told me about the love between him and Patrick:

Let's say that I loved him first, and then that I also loved the distance between us.

Something which, in a minor key, could also be said about our encounters.

A dream

Last night I dreamed that I went to Manoly's house again. It was late in the evening, sunset. The shadows of trees were falling heavily on the footpath. Dead leaves were everywhere; the garden was devoured by weeds. I couldn't find the door; the windows were empty holes. I dialed his number on my mobile: 9-6-6-2-4-9-7-1. His voice replied.

'Mr Lascaris, where are you?' I asked anxiously. 'I cannot find the door.'

'There is no door,' he replied.

'There is no door out of here. How am I to get in, then?' I said impatiently. But there was only silence. The prolonged metallic hum of an interrupted conversation.

Printed in Great Britain
by Amazon

13149121R00108